Space Legislation of Luxembourg

Aerospace Law and Policy Series

VOLUME 22

Editors

Pablo Mendes de Leon, Professor of Air and Space Law, and Tanja Masson-Zwaan, Assistant Professor of Space Law, Leiden University, The Netherlands.

Introduction

The *Aerospace Law and Policy Series* critically examines the fundamental changes that international aviation and space activities have undergone since the last century, growing up as mature industries while freeing themselves from traditional regulatory constraints and displaying a variety of innovative applications that call for creative legal solutions.

Objective

The objective of the Series is to make a contribution to legal thinking on public international air and space law and policy, and their implementation at the regional and national levels, responsibility and liability of public bodies and service providers, competition law, insurance law, company law, and the complex relationship between EU law and public international law.

Readership

Aviation and space lawyers, academics, representatives of governments, international organizations, and companies involved in aviation and space activities.

The titles published in this series are listed at the end of this volume.

Space Legislation of Luxembourg

A Commentary

Mahulena Hofmann
P.J. Blount
Gabrielle Leterre
Antonino Salmeri
Laetitia Zarkan

Wolters Kluwer

Published by:
Kluwer Law International B.V.
PO Box 316
2400 AH Alphen aan den Rijn
The Netherlands
E-mail: lrs-sales@wolterskluwer.com
Website: www.wolterskluwer.com/en/solutions/kluwerlawinternational

Sold and distributed by:
Wolters Kluwer Legal & Regulatory U.S.
7201 McKinney Circle
Frederick, MD 21704
United States of America
E-mail: customer.service@wolterskluwer.com

ISBN 978-94-035-4381-9

e-Book: ISBN 978-94-035-4391-8
web-PDF: ISBN 978-94-035-4401-4

Space Legislation of Luxembourg

A Commentary

Mahulena Hofmann
P.J. Blount
Gabrielle Leterre
Antonino Salmeri
Laetitia Zarkan

Wolters Kluwer

Published by:
Kluwer Law International B.V.
PO Box 316
2400 AH Alphen aan den Rijn
The Netherlands
E-mail: lrs-sales@wolterskluwer.com
Website: www.wolterskluwer.com/en/solutions/kluwerlawinternational

Sold and distributed by:
Wolters Kluwer Legal & Regulatory U.S.
7201 McKinney Circle
Frederick, MD 21704
United States of America
E-mail: customer.service@wolterskluwer.com

ISBN 978-94-035-4381-9

e-Book: ISBN 978-94-035-4391-8
web-PDF: ISBN 978-94-035-4401-4

Table of Contents

Foreword

For more than three decades, Luxembourg has been at the forefront of commercial and cooperative initiatives that have shaped a vibrant space economy. Today, the Grand Duchy is home to approximately seventy companies and research labs. The space sector's contribution to the nation's GDP is among the highest ratios in Europe.

In Luxembourg, the space industry finds a nurturing and supportive environment with an established community of high-tech businesses, researchers, and entrepreneurs along with access to the necessary services and facilities. As the pace of innovation in space-related technology continues to accelerate, making tomorrow's technical possibilities a reality requires practical and legal support today.

The end of the year 2020 was marked with an important achievement in enhancing the Luxembourg legal framework for space activities. On December 10, the Chamber of Deputies voted the Law on Space Activities and the Law on the Approval of the Convention on Registration of Objects Launched into Outer Space. The legislation responds to a growth and diversification of activities carried out in Luxembourg.

The Law on Space Activities and the Law of 2017 on the Exploration and Use of Space Resources are very important steps for Luxembourg and will be a valuable tool for further economic development of a dynamic and competitive space sector. It offers a clear legal framework for the authorization and supervision of space activities allowing the management of risks related to space activities and state liability as well as providing a safe and attractive environment for operators, investors and entrepreneurs.

The Law on Space Activities also establishes a National Register of Space Objects which shall include those objects for which Luxembourg assumes registration obligation under the Convention on Registration of Objects Launched into Outer Space. The national register is public and accessible to everyone on the Luxembourg Space Agency (LSA) website.

The LSA welcomes the idea of creating an academic Commentary on the three recent space laws of Luxembourg, explaining their *travaux préparatoires* and searching for the roots of the provisions, and is looking forward to this publication.

In Luxembourg, May 2022
Marc Serres, Chief Executive Officer, LSA

Introduction

In 2017, the Parliament of Luxembourg surprised the international space community by adopting a law enabling commercial missions to exploit space resources. In 2020, this act was followed by a general Law on Space Activities, which brought about a regime of authorization and supervision of all other space activities carried out under the jurisdiction of Luxembourg. At the same day of 2020, these legislative steps were completed by a law which allowed Luxembourg to ratify the 1975 Registration Convention.

This complex legislation, its mutual interplay and relation to the UN space treaties will influence the landscape of space activities not only in Luxembourg but also in other countries. It will be applied by Luxembourg's public institutions who will use it as a tool for organizing space business in the country. In the long term, the laws will be applied in domestic jurisprudence in cases of disputes. Such jurisprudence will interpret these provisions and determine in concrete cases whether the rules of the new space legislation were respected or violated and decide about the consequences. The laws are already object of academic interest, analyzed in the research and conferences and lectured in the Master courses at the University of Luxembourg and abroad. But foremost, they will be studied by the operators who are on the search for the most favorable jurisdiction for their space activities. As such, the laws will be the subject of keen interest to both start-ups and established companies, and their lawyers. They will evaluate whether the authorization procedure is smooth or cumbersome; affordable or expensive; and whether and which insurance is required; whether their potential liability for damage caused by their space object will be capped or not; and what will happen in case that they would be unable to continue their space activity. They will compare the effect of these legal acts with the foreign ones, weigh advantages against disadvantages, and decide.

As law operating with general terms cannot precisely determine all the details of potential future legal relations and procedures, the authors of this Commentary decided to go deeper into the legislative works and reveal the genesis of the provisions of the Luxembourg space laws leading to their final version. The principal reason of this exercise is to understand the core of the obligations and the circumstances of their adoption—or deletion from the text. This was seen as necessary also from the perspective of the fact that the crucial body influencing the final shape of the laws in Luxembourg, the Conseil d'État, several times recommended to delete provisions that it considered to be obvious or otherwise unnecessary. This was uncontestably a valid argument from the aspect of the legislative logic, but the resulting purity of some provisions of the text might bring an innocent reader to a puzzle requiring further explanation.

The second motive was the fact that according to Article 2 of the 1984 Language Act of Luxembourg, the only official language of the legislative acts in Luxembourg is French; this means that also the *travaux préparatoires* which—indeed—can be found on the website of the Parliament of Luxembourg, are accessible for those who master this wonderful and important language; for others they are not. The third ground was the temptation to profit from the experience the authors gained during their active participation in the preparation of the two of the three Drafts.

The original idea of the team was to comment the 2020 Law on Space Activities only. However, the cooperation with the Ministry of Economy and the Luxembourg Space Agency (LSA), which is now preparing the sub-statutory regulations, and the fact that the texts of the two space acts are highly harmonized, led to commenting both legal documents in a single volume. This starts with the 2017 Law on Space Resources, followed by the commentary on the 2020 Law on Space Activities of Luxembourg; at the end, a short commentary on the 2020 Law on the Approval of the Registration Convention can be found.

All texts commenting the articles follow the same structure: To facilitate working with the Commentary, all articles were given mostly unofficial short headings indicating their core content. They begin with the full text of the article, followed by its legislative history; after this part, the provision is interpreted. The last element is the evaluation of the rule accompanied by the comparison with examples coming from space laws of other countries. The shorter articles are evaluated in one text; the longer ones, which were developed in the course of the legislative works and sometimes have only a formal common denominator, are analyzed in a step-by-step approach. This structure was widely inspired by the Commentary on the *Building Blocks for the Development on an International Framework for the Governance of Space Resource Activities* published by the members of The Hague Space Resources Governance Working Group in 2020.

To simplify the work with the Commentary, the Annexes add the English translation of the texts of the laws. The translation of the first two Laws is based on the text published on the website of the LSA; the short Registration Law has been translated by the authors of the Commentary. To respect the authenticity of the translations, the text on the 2017 Law on Space Resources follows the term "minister" whereas the part discussing the 2020 Law operates with the form "Minister." The Commentary also chose the form "authorize" and "authorization" instead of "authorise" and "authorisation" because of the terms utilized by the Outer Space Treaty.

The work on the volume has been divided among the staff of the SES Chair in Space, SatCom and Media Law of the University of Luxembourg, who are experienced in several similar publications, including the *Commentary on The Hague Building*

Blocks (Eleven International 2020), *The Introduction to Space Law* (Wolters Kluwer 2019) or the UN e-course on Space Law, among others. P.J. Blount was postdoctoral researcher at the University of Luxembourg; Gabrielle Leterre, Antonino Salmeri, and Laetitia Zarkan are doctoral researchers at the SES Chair. The main editor is Mahulena Hofmann, holder of the SES Chair and regular lecturer at the Charles University in Prague, who had the chance to participate in the preparation of two of the three space laws included in this volume. The authors of the respective parts are indicated in the footnotes (*) to the Articles. A preliminary draft of this Commentary was presented in an international SES workshop, *National Legislation: Why, When and for Whom?*, on September 16, 2021 in Betzdorf.

Despite the fact that the result of this work is a moving target, pending the adoption of implementing rules and the practice, the authors of the Commentary still hope that they produced a useful tool for better understanding the space laws of Luxembourg. Only in discovering the relation of their numerous provisions with existing substantial and procedural legislation, they became aware of the complexity of the task, and will be grateful for recommendations on how this small text could be enhanced in the future. They thank all who supported the idea of the Commentary—especially the University of Luxembourg, the Luxembourg Space Agency, and SES.

In Luxembourg, May 2022
The authors

A Note on Citations

For ease, in this volume the authors have adopted consistent short citation forms for source materials that are cited repeatedly. These short citations are used in both text and the footnotes. The short citations are found below in bold.

Luxembourg Legislation

1991 Electronic Media Law—Loi du 27 juillet 1991 sur les médias électroniques, modifiée par Loi du 2 avril 2001, Mémorial A N° 88, 1er août 2001.

1993 Law on the Financial Sector—Loi du 5 avril 1993 relative au secteur financier telle qu'elle a été modifiée, Mémorial A N° 27, 10 avril 1993.

2017 Law on Space Resources—Loi du 20 juillet 2017 sur l'exploration et l'utilisation des ressources de l'espace, Mémorial A N° 674, 28 juillet 2017.

2020 Law on Space Activities—Loi du 15 décembre 2020 sur les activités spatiales, Mémorial A N° 1086, 28 décembre 2020.

Other Legislation

1993 South African Space Act—Space Affairs Act, No. 84, Article 13 (1993) (ZA).

2005 Belgian Space Law—The Law of September 17, 2005 (Belgian Official Journal of November 16, 2005) on the Activities of Launching, Flight Operation or Guidance of Space Objects.

2008 French Space Act—Loi N° 2008-518 du 3 juin 2008 relative aux opérations spatiales, No. 2008-518 (2008) (FR).

2006 Netherlands Space Activities Law—Rules Concerning Space Activities and the Establishment of a Registry of Space Objects (Space Activities Law).

2015 US CSLCA—Commercial Space Launch Competitiveness Act, 114 Pub. L. 90 (2015).

2018 UK Space Industry Act—Space Industry Act 2018, No. c. 5 (2018) (UK).

2019 UAE FLRSS—Federal Law No. 12 of 2019 on the Regulation of the Space Sector, entered into force January 20, 2020, 669 UAE Official Gazette 111 (2019).
2021 UK Space Industry Regulations—The Space Industry Regulations 2021, No. 797 (2021) (UK).
2021 Japan Space Resources Law—Act for Promotion of Business Activities Regarding Exploration and Exploitation of Space Resources of June 15, 2021.

International Legal Documents

Outer Space Treaty—Treaty on Principles Governing the Activities of States in the Exploration and Use of Outer Space, including the Moon and Other Celestial Bodies, entered into force on October 10, 1967, 18 U.S.T. 2410, 610 U.N.T.S. 205.
Liability Convention—Convention on International Liability for Damage Caused by Space Objects, entered into force on October 9, 1973, 961 U.N.T.S. 187.
Registration Convention—Convention on Registration of Objects Launched into Outer Space, entered into force on September 15, 1976, 1023 U.N.T.S. 15.

This volume has also sought to simply references to the preparatory materials referenced for each of the laws involved. All preparatory materials are available in full from the Luxembourg Parliamentary website. The below lists include the materials cited in this volume. A short citation form, indicated in bold, has been adopted for the Drafts of each law.

2017 Law on Space Resources

- **2016 Draft Law on Space Resources**—Saisine du Conseil d'État, November 15, 2016.
- Avis de la Chambre de Commerce (January 10, 2017).
- Avis du Conseil d'État (April 7, 2017).
- Chambre des Députés, Commission de l'Economie, Procès-verbal de la réunion du 4 mai 2017.
- Chambre des Députés, Commission de l'Economie, Procès-verbal de la réunion du 11 mai 2017.
- Chambre des Députés, Commission de l'Economie, Procès-verbal de la réunion du 18 mai 2017.
- Chambre des Députés, Commission de l'Economie, Procès-verbal de la réunion du 19 mai 2017.
- Dépêche du président de la Chambre des députés au président du Conseil d'État, May 24, 2017.
- Amendements parlementaires (May 24, 2017).
- Avis complémentaire de la Chambre de Commerce (June 13, 2017).
- Avis complémentaire du Conseil d'État (June 27, 2017).

- Chambre des Députés, Commission de l'Economie, Procès-verbal de la réunion du 29 juin 2017.
- Chambre des Députés, Commission de l'Economie, Procès-verbal de la réunion du 6 juillet 2017.
- Chambre des Députés, Rapport de la Commission de l'Economie (July 6, 2017).

2020 Law on Space Activities

- **2018 Draft Law on Space Activities**—Projet de loi sur les activités spatiales et portant modification de la loi modifiée du 9 juillet 1937 sur l'impôt sur les assurances, déposée le 12 juin 2018.
- Avis de la Chambre de Commerce (November 19, 2018).
- Avis du Conseil d'État (February 15, 2019).
- Chambre des Députés, Commission de l'Economie, de la Protection des consommateurs et de l'Espace, Procès-verbal de la réunion du 14 mai 2020.
- Chambre des Députés, Commission de l'Economie, de la Protection des consommateurs et de l'Espace; Commission de l'Environnement, du Climat, de l'Energie et de l'Aménagement du territoire, Procès-verbal de la réunion du 28 mai 2020.
- Chambre des Députés, Commission de l'Economie, de la Protection des consommateurs et de l'Espace; Commission des Classes moyennes et du Tourisme, Procès-verbal de la réunion du 11 juin 2020.
- Chambre des Députés, Commission de l'Economie, de la Protection des consommateurs et de l'Espace, Procès-verbal de la réunion du 18 juin 2020.
- Amendements parlementaires (July 20, 2020).
- Avis complémentaire du Conseil d'État (September 29, 2020).
- Chambre des Députés, Commission de l'Economie, de la Protection des consommateurs et de l'Espace, Procès-verbal de la réunion du 22 octobre 2020.
- Chambre des Députés, Commission de l'Economie, de la Protection des consommateurs et de l'Espace, Procès-verbal de la réunion du 2 décembre 2020.
- Rapport de la Commission de l'Economie, de la Protection des Consommateurs et de l'Espace (December 2, 2020).

CHAPTER 1 Commentary on the 2017 Law on Space Resources

Article 1 Ownership of Space Resources*

Space resources are capable of being owned.

I. DRAFTING HISTORY

In 2017, Luxembourg became the second country in the world—and the first in Europe—to pass legislation regulating commercial space resources activities.[1] Inspired by the space resources provisions contained in the US Commercial Space Launch Competitiveness Act (CSLCA)[2] passed in 2015 by the United States (US), in February 2016 the then Luxembourgish Minister of Economy, *Etienne Schneider*, launched the "spaceresources.lu initiative"[3] to transform Luxembourg into the European hub for space resource activities. Following the successful reception of the initiative, a "Draft Law on the Exploration and Use of Space Resources" was presented within the Luxembourgish Parliament to ensure that "private operators working in space can be confident about their rights to the resources they extract in outer space."[4] While the Parliament was debating the Draft, the Government signed two memoranda of understanding with foreign space mining companies—Deep Space Industries[5] and

* Antonino Salmeri

1. 2017 Law on Space Resources.
2. 2015 US CSLCA.
3. Luxembourg Space Agency, "Spaceresources.lu Initiative" (accessed June 2021) https://space-agency.public.lu/en/space-resources/the-initiative.html.
4. Luxembourg Ministry of Economy, "Luxembourg's New Space Law Guarantees Private Companies the Right to Resources Harvested in Outer Space in Accordance with International Law," *Business Wire* (November 11, 2016) https://www.businesswire.com/news/home/20161111005294/en/Luxembourg%E2%80%99s-New-Space-Law-Guarantees-Private-Companies-the-Right-to-Resources-Harvested-in-Outer-Space-in-Accordance-with-International-Law.
5. Luxembourg Ministry of Economy, "Luxembourg Government and Deep Space Industries Sign MoU," *Business Wire* (May 5, 2016) https://www.businesswire.com/news/home/20160505005655/en/Luxembourg-Government-Deep-Space-Industries-Sign-MoU. It should be noted that Deep Space Industry ceased to be a mining company and was acquired by Bradford Space in 2019. Jeff Foust, "Deep Space Industries Acquired by Bradford Space," *Space News* (January 2, 2019) https://spacenews.com/deep-space-industries-acquired-by-bradford-space/.

iSpace[6]—for the establishment of their European subsidiaries in the Grand Duchy.[7] Finally, on August 1, 2017 the *Loi du 20 juillet 2017 sur l'exploration et l'utilisation des ressources de l'espace*—"Law of July 20, 2017, on the Exploration and Use of Space Resources"—entered into force, inaugurating the domestic regulatory framework for space resource activities.[8] It is important to note that when it enacted this Law, Luxembourg did not have any general legislation governing private activities in space except for the 1991 Electronic Media Law.[9] Four years later, this gap has been closed with the enactment of the 2020 Law on Space Activities, which applies to all space activities under the jurisdiction of Luxembourg except for space resources missions.

The original text of the 2017 Law on Space Resources[10] has been thoroughly scrutinized by the Luxembourgish Conseil d'État—an institution which advises the national legislature—in its opinion of April 7, 2017.[11] This scrutiny was preceded by some general considerations on the object and purpose of the Law on Space Resources. The Conseil's analysis began by summarizing the applicable international framework[12] and recalling the provisions of the 2015 US CSLCA,[13] to better evaluate the broader context around the 2017 Law. Following this, the Conseil moved to consider whether, in this given context, this Law is able to reach its declared purpose, which is to provide legal certainty to private actors interested in investing and/or conducting space resource activities.[14] Throughout its analysis, the Conseil presented a series of questions and expresses some doubts, the first one being how could Luxembourg ensure that foreign States will recognize the resource rights granted under the Law on Space Resources.[15] This issue was particularly critical for the Conseil given that almost all activities related to space resources—from launching the relevant mission to extracting, refining, and commercializing the resources—will take place outside Luxembourg's territory and control. For instance, the Conseil wondered how Luxembourg could guarantee its operators against the risk of having their extracted resources confiscated by foreign authorities holding a different interpretation of international space law. Furthermore, the Conseil seriously questioned the ability of Luxembourg to

6. Luxembourg Ministry of Economy, "Luxembourg and ispace, a Tokyo-Based Lunar Robotic Exploration Company, Sign MoU to Co-Operate within the Spaceresources.lu Initiative," *Business Wire* (May 5, 2016) https://www.businesswire.com/news/home/20170302005800/en/Luxembourg-ispace-Tokyo-Based-Lunar-Robotic-Exploration-Company.
7. Notably, these memoranda of understanding were concluded on top of a conspicuous financial investment in another space mining company called Planetary Resources, which also ceased its activities after being acquired by a blockchain firm. Peter de Selding, "Luxembourg Taking Major Stake in Planetary Resources' European Business," *Space News* (June 13, 2016) https://spacenews.com/luxembourg-government-to-buy-up-to-49-of-planetary-resources-european-business/ and Jeff Foust, "Asteroid Mining Company Planetary Resources Acquired by Blockchain Firm," *Space News* (October 13, 2018) https://spacenews.com/asteroid-mining-company-planetary-resources-acquired-by-blockchain-firm/.
8. 2017 Law on Space Resources.
9. 1991 Electronic Media Law.
10. 2016 Draft Law on Space Resources.
11. Avis du Conseil d'État du 7 avril 2017, 8.
12. *Id.* at 1-3.
13. *Id.* at 4.
14. *Id.* at 5.
15. *Id.*

safeguard the material conduct of the authorized space resource activities in the absence of any legitimate sovereign authority over celestial bodies.[16] Based on these arguments, the Conseil concluded that due to the lack of supporting regulation at the international level, the Law on Space Resources could not meet its purpose of providing legal certainty to private actors concerning space resource activities.[17] However, as can be seen from the adoption of the law by the Parliament by the overwhelming majority of the deputies,[18] this issue can be seen also differently.

The original text of Article 1 of the 2017 Law on Space Resources read that "space resources are capable of being owned in accordance with international law."[19] This formulation was later amended by the Commission of Economy of the Parliament pursuant to the comments of the Conseil.[20] On the one hand, the Conseil noted that Article 1 could not provide that "space resources are capable of being owned in accordance with international law" because Luxembourg has no competence to declare what is legal under international law.[21] On the other hand, if the purpose was to commit the declaration to comply with the international law, the Conseil found the provision superfluous given that this compliance automatically follows from the hierarchical status of international law in the constitutional system of Luxembourg.[22] On this note, the Conseil suggested to follow the example set by the CSLCA, which rather references the international obligations of the State. Based on the above reasoning, the Conseil recommended to drop the declaration on the appropriability of space resources and consequently to suppress Article 1 of the Draft.[23] Notwithstanding this opinion of the Conseil, the Commission decided to keep Article 1 of the Draft, to maintain in the law an unequivocal statement concerning the appropriability of space resources.[24] At the same time, the Commission recognized the importance of international regulation and called for the development of a new multilateral instrument complementing the provisions of the Outer Space Treaty (OST).[25] On a similar line of reasoning, the Commission acknowledged the need to refer to and respect Luxembourg's international obligations, as pointed out by the Conseil, and amended the following Article 2 to this end.[26]

II. INTERPRETATION

Article 1 of the Law on Space Resources declares that "space resources are capable of being owned" (in French: *les ressources de l'espace sont susceptibles d'appropriation*).[27]

16. *Id.*
17. *Id.* at 6.
18. Bulletin de vote, PL 7093, 13 juillet 2017; Oui 55, Abst 0, Non 2, Total 57.
19. Avis du Conseil d'État du 7 avril 2017, 4.
20. Amendements parlementaires (May 24, 2017) 2.
21. Avis du Conseil d'État du 7 avril 2017, 7.
22. *Id.*
23. *Id.* at 8.
24. Amendements parlementaires (May 24, 2017) 2-3.
25. *Id.*
26. 2016 Draft Law on Space Resources, 4.
27. Amendements parlementaires (May 24, 2017) 2-3.

As recalled above, the purpose of this provision is to provide private actors with legal certainty concerning the legitimate conduct of space resource activities. In line with the reasoning put forward by the Commission of Economy,[28] Article 1 of the 2017 Law on Space Resources can fulfill this purpose as a critical element of an integrated approach which includes measures at both national and international level.

Under Article I of the OST, celestial bodies shall be free for exploration and use by all States.[29] Pursuant to Article 31 of the Vienna Convention on the Law of Treaties,[30] the interpretation of "use" under Article I OST encompasses a variety of activities, both of commercial and scientific nature,[31] including those related to their resources. In this respect, it is important to note that space resource activities have actually been among the very first endeavors ever conducted by States on celestial bodies[32] and represent a critical element for the sustainability of space missions.[33] This interpretation is also in line with Article II OST, which lays down the prohibition of national appropriation of celestial bodies.[34] According to this provision, States are forbidden from extending their sovereign influence over outer space and celestial bodies by means of their territorial annexation.[35] So long as these effects are avoided, Article II OST does not prevent States from using celestial bodies for the purpose of extracting, recovering or using their space resources.[36]

Article 1 of the Law constitutes a legitimate interpretation of the freedom to explore and use celestial bodies in compliance with the prohibition of national appropriation under Articles I and II of the OST.[37] Contrary to the opinion expressed by the Conseil, Luxembourg is entitled to put forward such interpretation in its national legislation as part of its sovereign right to interpret ambiguous provisions of international law.[38] At the same time, it is true that declaring the legality of space resource activities does not necessarily suffice to provide private actors with the level of legal

28. *Id.*
29. Outer Space Treaty, Art. I.
30. Vienna Convention on the Law of Treaties, entered into force on January 27, 1980, 1155 U.N.T.S. 331.
31. Tanja Masson-Zwaan, "Article VI of the Outer Space Treaty and Private Human Access to Space," in *Proceedings of the 51st Colloquium on the Law of Outer Space* (AIAA 2009) 537.
32. *See generally* NASA, "Apollo 11 Mission Overview" (January 5, 2022) https://www.nasa.gov/mission_pages/apollo/missions/apollo11.html; NASA, "Soviet Union Lunar Sample Return Missions" (March 16, 2010) https://www.nasa.gov/mission_pages/LRO/multimedia/lroimages/lroc-20100316-luna.html.
33. Jim Brindestine, "Space Resources Are the Key to Safe and Sustainable Lunar Exploration," NASA (September 10, 2020) https://blogs.nasa.gov/bridenstine/2020/09/10/space-resources-are-the-key-to-safe-and-sustainable-lunar-exploration/.
34. Outer Space Treaty, Art. II.
35. P.J. Blount, "Outer Space and International Geography: Article II and the Shape of the Global Order," *New England Law Review* 52(2) (2018) 102-103.
36. Mahulena Hofmann & Tanja Masson-Zwaan, *Introduction to Space Law* (2019) 99. *See also* International Institute of Space Law, "Position Paper on Space Resources Mining" (Dec. 20, 2015).
37. Mahulena Hofmann, "Space Resources: Regulatory Aspects, in: Mahulena Hofmann & P.J. Blount eds., *Innovation in Outer Space: International and African Legal Perspectives* (Nomos 2018) 202-203.
38. Antonino Salmeri, "The Integration Between National and International Regulation of Space Resources Activities Under Public International Law," *Journal of Space Law*, 43(1) (2019) 60-85.

certainty needed to invest in their conduct. Questions related to the international recognition of property rights as well as to the protection of space resource activities against harmful interference naturally require a certain level of international harmonization and coordination. Since 2016, these and other related topics came under the consideration of the Legal Subcommittee of the United Nations Committee on the Peaceful Uses of Outer Space. After some years of general discussion, during its 60th Session in June 2021 the subcommittee agreed to the establishment of a working group on space resource activities.[39] Within this context, Article 1 of the Law on Space Resources has notably contributed to bringing the regulation of space resource activities to the attention of the international community for the purpose of developing adequate regulation.

III. EVALUATION

Currently, only three other countries have enacted national legislation on space resource activities: the US,[40] the United Arab Emirates (UAE),[41] and Japan.[42] When compared to its homologues, the language used in Article 1 of the 2017 Law on Space Resources of Luxembourg—*les ressources de l'espace sont susceptibles d'appropriation*—is rather short and straightforward. In this respect, it is important to underline that Article 1 of the Law should always be read in connection with the following Article 2. This is because following the comments received from the Conseil, the Chamber of Deputies decided to move the reference assuring compliance with international law in a new paragraph within Article 2.[43]

In the US, section 402 of Title IV of the 2015 US CSLCA carefully avoids the use of the term "appropriation" and broadly refers to the right of US citizens "engaged in commercial recovery of space resources ... to possess, own, transport, use, and sell it according to applicable law, including U.S. international obligations."[44] In the UAE, Article 4 of the 2019 Federal Law on the Regulation of the Space Sector (FLRSS) includes "space resources exploration or extraction activities," as well as "activities for the exploitation and use of space resources for scientific, commercial or other purposes" among the activities permitted and regulated in the UAE.[45] However, Article 18 defers the decision concerning "the conditions and controls" affecting such activities to future administrative provisions to be enacted by the Council of Ministers.[46] Despite some editorial differences in language and drafting, Article 1 of the Luxembourg law is

39. Report of the Legal Subcommittee on its 60th session, held in Vienna from May 31 to June 11, 2021, U.N. Doc. A/AC.105/1243 (2021). The exact mandate and terms of reference for the group was finalized at the Plenary Session in August 2021.
40. 2015 US CSLCA.
41. 2019 UAE FLRSS.
42. The Japan Space Resources Law has been passed by the Japanese Diet on June 15, 2021. Due to the current lack of an English translation, the provisions of this Law will not be considered in the analysis of this Article.
43. Amendements parlementaires (May 24, 2017) 2-3.
44. 2015 US CSLCA, s. 402, § 51303.
45. 2019 UAE FLRSS, Art. 4.
46. *Id.* at Art. 18.

aligned with these other laws and contributes to the same goal: providing legal certainty on space resource activities in compliance with international law.

Finally, Article 1 of the 2017 Law on Space Resources can also be connected with section 10 of the Artemis Accords, a multilateral document released in October 2020 that lays down "Principles for Cooperation in the Civil Exploration and Use of the Moon, Mars, Comets and Asteroids for Peaceful Purposes."[47] Acknowledging the critical importance of space resources for sustainable space exploration, the Signatories to the Accords—at present, nineteen States including Luxembourg—affirm the compatibility of space resource activities with the OST and commit to conduct them in compliance with the provisions of the Treaty.[48] Evidently, provisions like Article 1 of the 2017 Law on Space Resources or section 402 of the 2015 US CSLCA have played a central role in paving the way for these new developments at the multilateral level.

47. The Artemis Accords—Principles for Cooperation in the Civil Exploration and Use of the Moon, Mars, Comets, and Asteroids for Peaceful Purposes (October 13, 2020).
48. *Id.* at s. 10.

Article 2 Mission Authorization

The text of Article 2 is composed of several provisions which were introduced in different stages of the preparation of the Draft and do not necessarily cover the same subject matter. The first paragraph prohibits the performance of space resource activities under Luxemburg's jurisdiction without a formal authorization, and the second paragraph deals with the transparency of third-party agency of the operator. The third part underlines the necessity of carrying out space resource activities in accordance with international law, whereas the fourth provision exempts satellite communication from the material scope of the law. Due to this complexity, the four paragraphs are commented separately.

(1) No person can explore or use space resources without holding a written mission authorization from the minister or ministers in charge of the economy and space activities (hereinafter "the ministers").[*]

I. DRAFTING HISTORY

The provision that no one can explore or use space resources without holding a written mission authorization from the minister or ministers in charge of economy and space activities can be found already in the original version of this Article.[1] The 2016 Commentary on Articles accompanying the text of the 2016 Draft Law on Space Resources[2] underlined that the obligation to authorize national space activities flows from Article VI of the 1967 OST. On the national level, this rule has been extensively inspired by Article 2(1) of the 1993 Law on the Financial Sector.[3]

---

* Mahulena Hofmann

1. 2016 Draft Law on Space Resources.
2. *See* the English Translation of the 2016 Draft Law on Space Resources, available at https://gouvernement.lu/dam-assets/fr/actualites/communiques/2016/11-novembre/11-presentation-spaceresources/Draft-law-space_press.pdf (accessed November 29, 2021).
3. 1993 Law on Financial Sector, pp. 462 ff. (*Aucune personne de droit luxembourgeois ne peut exercer l'activité d'établissement de crédit sans être en possession d'un agrément écrit du ministre ayant dans ses attributions de 'Commission de surveillance du secteur financier.*)

This obligation is applicable to space resource activities, which are the exploration and use of space resources for commercial purposes.[4] However, contrary to the 2015 US CSLCA, neither the 2016 Draft Law on Space Resources nor its 2017 final version includes any definition of "space resources." Only the Explanatory Statement to the 2016 Draft[5] states that space resources are "nowadays commonly defined as abiotic resources that can be found in situ in outer space and that can be extracted"; according to the Statement, this definition includes for example mineral resources and water, but not the "orbital positions or frequency spectrum."[6] Furthermore, this document adds that the use of "resources" in the Draft does not address "asteroids, comets, or celestial bodies themselves."[7]

The lack of definition of space resources was commented on by the Chamber of Commerce—a public institution that intervenes in the legislative procedure—in its statement of January 2017.[8] The Chamber observed that a definition would help future operators to better orientate in the legal setup. A similar position was taken in the 2017 Opinion of the Conseil d'État.[9] After having quoting the 2015 US CSLCA,[10] which defines "asteroid resources"[11] and "space resources,"[12] the Conseil recommended that some or similar definitions should be included also in the law of Luxembourg.[13] The Commission of Economy of the Parliament reacted on this Opinion in May 2017 not with a positive definition of space resources but with a new paragraph of the coordinated text of the Draft.[14] This new paragraph exempted satellite communication from the scope of the law. This solution entered the final text of the Law.[15]

The notion "exploration and use" of space resources in Article 2 of the Law follows the terminology of Article I of the OST. However, according to the 2016 Commentary on Articles, it does not cover the legal regimes of launching activities and the launched objects needed for the resources. The launching activities must be subject to a separate authorization, and the registration of space objects should be subject of distinct rules.[16] For the sake of transparency, the Chamber of Commerce recommended an inclusion of provisions exempting the launch activities from space resources authorizations in the body of the Law.[17] These discussions resulted in the more general Article 17 of the 2017 Law on Space Resources, which explains that the authorization

4. 2017 Law on Space Resources, Art. 3.
5. English Translation of the 2016 Draft Law on Space Resources.
6. *See also* the results of the Hague International Space Resources Governance Working Group in: Olavo de Bittencourt Neto, Mahulena Hofmann, Tanja Masson-Zwaan, and Dimitra Stefoudi, *Building Blocks for the Development of an International Framework for the Governance of Space Resources Activities: A Commentary* (Eleven 2020) 157.
7. 2016 Draft Law on Space Resources, 7.
8. Avis de la Chambre de Commerce (January 10, 2017).
9. Avis du Conseil d'État (April 7, 2017).
10. 2015 US CSLCA.
11. "[A] space resource found on or within a single asteroid." *Id.* at s. 402.
12. "[A]n abiotic resource in situ in outer space," which "includes water and minerals." *Id.*
13. According to the 2019 UAE FLRSS, space resources are any non-living resources present in outer space, including minerals and water.
14. Amendements parlementaires (May 24, 2017).
15. Rapport de la Commission de l'économie (July 6, 2017).
16. English Translation of the 2016 Draft Law on Space Resources.
17. Avis du Conseil d'État (April 7, 2017).

for a mission does not dispense operators from the need to obtain other approvals or authorizations.

The Conseil d'État opened the question of extent of the term "use" of space resources, especially in view of "commercialization." Specifically, the Conseil asked whether the Law, including the obligation for authorization, should also cover the purchase of space resources from operators who brought them to the Earth by third persons, the transformation of such resources, and the sale of space resources. Would the acquirer be bound by the Law on Space Resources and would he/she need authorization for such activities under this Law? In its Opinion, the Conseil recommended that only the entity that carries out the mission and brings the resources to the Earth is subject of the authorization procedure. Any other solution, such as an obligation of the person acquiring directly or indirectly space resources to apply for the authorization would collide with the European law protecting the free circulation of goods.[18] The Commission of Economy confirmed the position of the Conseil by the statement that the term "use" of space resources does not include the acquirement of space resources.[19]

It may be confusing that, on the one hand, the "commercialization" of space resources is exempted from the scope of the Law, but on the other hand, according to Article 3 of the 2017 Law on Space Resources, the authorization procedure is required only if the space resources mission is carried out for "commercial purposes." Missions that are not commercial in nature are not subject to this Law but may be covered by the 2020 general Law on Space Activities. The 2016 Commentary on Articles gave examples of such noncommercial missions, including scientific missions or activities for "purely private purposes." However, what are the missions for commercial purposes that do not entail the commercialization of space resources? It can be guessed that they are the missions *leading* to the commercialization of other activities in space. Space resources can be sold and bought; but the 2017 Law on Space Resources purposely does not regulate this element of the chain, perhaps with the exception of Article 1, which proclaims that space resources are capable to be owned. The Opinion of the Conseil d'État reminds on the fact that similar approach was chosen by the 2015 US CSLCA which limited its scope to the commercial exploration and commercial recovery of space resources (§ 51302).[20]

The term "authorization" will be interpreted in the part dealing with Articles 4-12 of the Law. The term "mission" applied in Article 2(1) is not defined in the 2017 Law, and logically also neither its duration. The original provision of the 2016 Draft stating that the authorization shall be granted for a "specific period" and is renewable (former Article 5) was analogous to Article 20 of the 1991 Electronic Media Law. Surprisingly, in the general term "specific period," the Conseil d'État saw a violation of the freedom of commerce guaranteed by Article 11 paragraph 6 of the Constitution of

18. Avis du Conseil d'État (April 7, 2017) 10.
19. Amendements parlementaires (May 24, 2017).
20. The 2019 UAE FLRSS covers space resources exploration or extraction activities, as well as activities for the exploitation and use of space resources for scientific, commercial or other purposes.

Luxembourg.[21] According to the Conseil, the duration of the mission should be determined by the applicant and assessed by the minister during the authorization procedure.[22] Consequently, the "specific period" provision was deleted from the text.

According to Article 2(1) of the 2017 Law on Space Resources, the authorization shall be granted by one or two ministers—the one responsible for the economy and another one for space activities. This provision corresponds to the drafting period of the Law. The Ministry of State and its Service of Communication and Media had traditionally been in charge of authorizing SES satellites, whereas the Ministry of Economy was engaged in building up its competences mostly in the New Space sector. The Conseil d'État found the involvement of two ministers in the authorization progress of space resources missions cumbersome as the Law remained open as to which of the two ministers a future operator should address the application. Instead, the Opinion of the Conseil recommended vesting the decision process in one Ministry coupled with a consultation with other ministers of the Government of Luxembourg as needed.

This double competence was also the subject of the debates of the parliamentary Commission on Economy.[23] Pragmatically, the Commission stressed that this situation may be changed through redactional modifications of the Law in the future.

The parliamentary elections in 2018 brought about changes in the composition of the Government and in the ministerial competences.[24] The Ministry of Economy was charged with the legislation on space activities and their authorization. The Ministry of State and its Media and Communication Service kept its competences in regulating the satellite systems of Luxembourg, the supervision of SES, and the management of radio frequency spectrum. However, at the time of writing this commentary, the double competence provision of the 2017 Law on Space Resources was unchanged.[25]

II. INTERPRETATION

The 2017 Law on Space Resources is limited to the authorization of defined space resources missions that are carried out for commercial purposes. The hurdle for obtaining an authorization for such commercial missions is relatively high. It is bound on numerous conditions enumerated in Articles 4-14. The sanctions for starting a space resources mission or attempting to do so without authorization are more than tangible. Such behavior will be punished by imprisonment of between eight days and five years and a fine of between EUR 5,000 and EUR 1,250,000 or either one of those penalties (Article 18(1)).

The authorization fulfills several functions. At the level of international law, it implements Article VI of the OST. At the domestic level, it has the role of an

21. Constitution coordonnée du Grand-Duché de Luxembourg, Mémorial A N° 23, 22 octobre 1868.
22. Avis du Conseil d'État (April 7, 2017) 13.
23. Chambre des Députés, Commission de l'Economie, Procès-verbal de la réunion du 11 mai 2017.
24. Arrêté grand-ducal du 5 décembre 2018 portant constitution des Ministères.
25. The double competence was not made a part of the 2020 Law on Space Activities.

administrative act following the corresponding administrative procedure.[26] Analogous to the 2020 Law on Space Activities, the form of the decision should be a "ministerial order" (*arrêté ministeriel*).[27] On a different level, it has been also discussed whether a successful authorization can be seen as a label of credibility of the authorized private operators and lead, in case of their bankruptcy, to financial claims of those who financed the mission against the State. This interpretation was rejected by the representative of the Ministry of Economy with the reference to the condition of sufficient financial means of the operators needed for the successful authorization.[28]

Whereas the form of an authorization is defined by the 2020 Law on Space Activities as "ministerial order," the form of a refusal of the application for authorization is not specified by the space laws. Theoretically, the form of such administrative decision can constitute an individual or normative act issued by the minister. Both can be appealed, and reviewed by the administrative jurisdiction of Luxembourg, the individual administrative act as object of an appeal for annulment (*recours en annulation*) and appeal for reversal (*recours en réformation*), the normative act as object of appeal for annulment.[29] In practice, the form of an individual administrative act may prevail.

It is interesting to compare the procedures leading to the authorization of space resources mission with the principal model for the 2017 Law on Space Resources, the 1993 Law on Financial Sector.[30] An application to carry on the business of a credit institution from the minister responsible for the Commission for Supervision of the Financial Sector must be supported by a statement of the reasons on which it is based. In contrast to the 2017 Law on Space Resources, it contains specific deadlines for the decision. The decision must be notified to the applicant within six months of receipt of the application or, if the application is incomplete, within six months of receipt of the information needed for the adoption of the decision. Such a decision shall in any event be adopted within twelve months of receipt of the application, failing which the absence of a decision shall be deemed to constitute notification of a decision refusing the application. An appeal against the decision may be lodged within one month and may be struck out if it is not so lodged, before administrative court,[31] which shall determine the matter as a court adjudicating on the substance.

26. Loi réglant la procédure administrative non contentieuse, Mémorial A N° 87, 27 décembre 1978; Règlement grand-ducal relatif à la procédure à suivre par les administrations relevant de l'État et des communes, Mémorial A N° 54, 6 juillet 1979.
27. 2020 Law on Space Activities, Art. 5(3).
28. Chambre des Députés, Commission de l'Economie, Procès-verbal de la réunion du 11 mai 2017, 3.
29. *See* the Law of June 21, 1999 Concerning the Procedural Rules in Administrative Courts (the 1999 Act), Mémorial N° 98, 26 juillet 1999, Art. 13(1) (dealing with the individual acts) and Art. 16 (dealing with the normative acts).
30. 1993 Law on Financial Sector.
31. Law of November 7, 1996 on the Organisation of Administrative Courts and Tribunals (Mémorial A 1996, p. 2261) Art. 100.

III. EVALUATION

The requirement to obtain an authorization for space resources mission can be found in the predecessor of the Luxembourg Law on Space Resources, the 2015 US CSLCA. According to § 51320 of the 2015 US law, space mining actors have to obtain an authorization from the US authorities. As a preliminary measure, this Law required the US President to submit to Congress a report determining a specific process of authorization of commercial exploitation of space resources since existing authorization procedures were not applicable to space mining activities. As there is no specific federal agency with authority to authorize space resources activities (as of yet), the President's report endorsed using, as a temporary solution, an "enhanced" version of the Federal Aviation Administration's payload review process to authorize such missions.[32] The procedure is based on interagency cooperation, especially with the Department of State and is limited to procedural aspects of mission authorization.[33]

The 2019 UAE FLRSS considers "space resources exploration or extraction activities" as "regulated activities" requiring an authorization by the UAE Space Agency.[34] According to Article 18 of this Law, the conditions relating to permits for the exploration, exploitation and use of space resources, including their acquisition, purchase, sale, trade, transportation, storage, and any space activities aimed at providing logistical services in this regard shall be determined by a decision issued by the Council of Ministers or whomever it delegates. The permit shall be granted by a decision of the Board of Directors of the Agency upon the proposal of the Director General.

According to the Japanese Space Resources Mining Law, a governmental permit is required to pursue space mining activity.[35]

The provision of Article 2 of the 2017 Law on Space Resources gives the Luxembourg Government the means to decide whether an operator fulfills the criteria enumerated in the Law, and it offers the operators the guarantee that their activities are legal from the perspective of the Luxembourgish legal system. Despite the plural reference to "ministries," according to the 2018 Decree on the Establishment of Ministries, the authorization of a space resources mission will be granted by the Minister of Economy, but the Ministry of State must be contacted if radio frequencies allocated to Luxembourg will be needed for the mission.[36]

(2) No person shall be authorized to carry out the activity referred to in paragraph 1 either through another person or as an intermediary for the carrying out of such activity.

32. Tanja Masson-Zwaan and Neta Palkovicz, "Regulation of Space Resources Rights: Meeting the Needs of States and Private Parties," *QIL* 35(5) (2017) 11-12.
33. Joanne J. Gabrynowicz, "Title IV of the 2015 U.S. Commercial Space Launch Competitiveness Act," Presentation at the IISL/ECSL Symposium on Space Law (March 27, 2017) http://www.unoosa.org/documents/pdf/copuos/lsc/2017/symp-05.pdf.
34. 2019 UAE FLRSS.
35. 2021 Japan Space Resources Law.
36. Arrêté grand-ducal du 5 décembre 2018 portant constitution des Ministères.

The provision that no person shall be authorized to carry out the activity referred in paragraph 1 either through another person or as an intermediary for carrying out such activity was not part of the original 2016 Draft. The Conseil d'État recommended that for the sake of transparency as to third-party control of an operator, this provision should be reproduced from the 1993 Law on Financial Sector (Article 2 paragraph 2). It found its way into the text of the 2017 Law through the final Draft submitted by the Commission on Economy on July 6, 2017[37] and became unchanged part of the adopted Law.

(3) The authorized operator may only carry out the activity referred to in paragraph 1 in accordance with the conditions of the authorization and the international obligations of Luxembourg.[*]

I. DRAFTING HISTORY

Article 2 appeared originally in the Draft Law with a shorter text, which provided that no person could engage in the exploration or use of space resources without the previous written agreement of the ministers in charge of economy and space. Pursuant to the Opinion of the Conseil,[38] this provision has undergone various amendments. In its opinion, the Conseil noted that the freedom to explore and use space resources cannot be unlimited. Therefore, authorized operators must conduct their activities in compliance with the conditions of their authorization, as well as with the international obligations of Luxembourg. This suggestion has been implemented by the parliamentary Commission of Economy with the addition of the new paragraph 3.

II. INTERPRETATION

Article 2(3) of the 2017 Law on Space Resources obliges operators to conduct space resource activities in accordance with the conditions of their authorization and the international obligations of Luxembourg. It is important to note that this provision is further complemented by Article 15 of this Law, according to which "the minister(s) authorizing a space resource mission are also in charge of its continuous supervision."[39] The main purpose of Article 2(3) is to implement the international obligations of Luxembourg as a Party to the OST and specifically the obligations stemming from its Articles III and VI.

Article VI OST establishes the international responsibility of States for their national space activities.[40] According to this provision, private activities in outer space shall require the authorization and continuing supervision of the appropriate State,

37. Rapport de la Commission de l'économie (July 6, 2017) 9.
* Antonino Salmeri
38. Avis du Conseil d'État (April 7, 2017).
39. 2017 Law on Space Resources, Art. 15.
40. Michael Gerhard, "Article VI," in Stephan Hobe, Bernhard Schmidt-Tedd and Kai-Uwe Schrogl eds., *Cologne Commentary on Space Law: Vol. 1* (2009) 105.

which shall assure their conformity with the provisions of the Treaty.[41] It is important to note that under Article VI OST these obligations are guaranteed by the international responsibility of the State,[42] which entails that their violation would likely constitute an internationally wrongful act.[43]

Article 2(3) of the 2017 Law on Space Resources implements the obligations stemming from Article VI of the OST for those that concern the duty to authorize. Accordingly, Article 2(1) of the 2017 Law provides that the exploration and use of space resources can only be conducted with the written authorization from the competent ministers. To complement this obligation, Article 2(3) requires operators to further conform to the conditions stated in the authorization throughout the entirety of the mission. As mentioned, compliance with the duty to supervise under Article VI OST is ensured by Article 15 of the Law, according to which the same ministers authorizing the mission will also be responsible for—and in charge of—its continuing supervision.

Article 2(3) of the 2017 Law on Space Resources also implements the obligations laid down in Article III of the OST, which establishes the applicability of international law in outer space, within the authorization procedure for space resource activities.[44] According to Article III of the OST, all space activities shall be conducted "in accordance with international law, including the Charter of the United Nations, in the interest of maintaining international peace and security and promoting international cooperation and understanding."[45] This provision harmonizes the regulation of space activities with the legal order of international law and has a fundamental role in preserving outer space as a peaceful and cooperative domain.[46] In accordance with Article III of the OST, the second part of Article 2(3) subjects the valid conduct of the authorized space resource activity to comply with Luxembourg's international obligations. Pursuant to this clause, any operator conducting its space resource activity in violation of these international obligations would also breach its duties under Article 2(3). Consequently, the operator may be fined under Article 18 of the 2017 Law and could also be obliged to indemnify the Grand Duchy of Luxembourg in case the latter had to reparate or compensate any damage caused.

III. EVALUATION

Comparing Article 2(3) of the 2017 Law on Space Resources with the 2015 US CSLCA, specifically section 402 of Title IV, this provision specifically mentions the international obligations of the US among the conditions affecting the right of US citizens to engage

41. Outer Space Treaty, Art. VI.
42. *Id.*
43. Under the Articles on State Responsibility for Internationally Wrongful Acts. UN General Assembly, Resolution 56/83: Responsibility of States for Internationally Wrongful Acts. The consolidated text as adopted by UNGA Resolution 56/83 and corrected by UN DOC A/56/49(Vol. I)/Corr.4.
44. Olivier Ribbelink, "Article III," in Stephan Hobe, Bernhard Schmidt-Tedd & Kai-Uwe Schrogl eds., *Cologne Commentary on Space Law: Vol. 1* (2009) 64-69.
45. Outer Space Treaty, Art. III.
46. Bin Cheng, *Studies in International Space Law* (2004) 150-211.

in space resource activities. This reference is further complemented by the declaration laid down in section 403, according to which "the US does not thereby assert sovereignty or sovereign or exclusive rights or jurisdiction over, or the ownership of, any celestial body."[47] For what concerns the 2019 UAE FLRSS, none of the provisions referring to space resource activities—Articles 4 and 18—include any mention of compliance with relevant international obligations. However, this is most likely since the "conditions and controls" applicable to space resource activities will be laid down in future administrative regulation by the UAE Council of Ministers.[48]

When compared to the above homologue provisions in the US and UAE legislation, Article 2(3) of the 2017 Law on Space Resources strikes a good balance between the more careful approach of the 2015 US CSLCA and the minimalistic one of the 2019 UAE FLRSS. To this end, the provision sufficiently clarifies the willingness of Luxembourg to prioritize respect of its international obligations over operators' claims in the conduct of space resource activities.

(4) This Law shall not apply to satellite communications, orbital positions, or the use of frequency bands.*

I. DRAFTING HISTORY

After Article 2(1) positively determines the scope of the 2017 Law on Space Resources—the Law is applicable if the activity deals with "space resources," and specifically, the "exploration and use" of space resources when this exploration and use are "for commercial purposes." Article 2(4) serves as a partial negative determination of the scope of the 2017 Law.

The provision which exempts satellite communication from the scope of the Law on Space Resources was not involved in the 2016 Draft. This rule was included on the initiative of the Conseil d'État which required that satellite communication was clearly exempted from the material scope of the Law, because the establishment and operation of Luxembourg satellite systems are regulated by the 1991 Electronic Media Law. This 1991 Law defines "Luxembourg satellite systems" as any system of one or more satellites using the satellite frequencies of the Grand Duchy of Luxembourg (Article 2). According to Article 20 of this Law, nobody can establish and operate a Luxembourgish satellite system without previously having obtained a concession, granted by the Government. The conditions for obtaining the concessions are enumerated in this Law.

The specific function of the 1991 Electronic Media Law and the system of concessions was underlined in the debates of the parliamentary Commission of Economy.[49] The Commission recommended that additional forms of using outer space are exempted from the scope of the 2017 Law on Space Resources, such as refueling or

47. 2015 US CSLCA, s. 403.
48. 2019 UAE FLRSS, Art. 18.
* Mahulena Hofmann
49. Chambre des Députés, Commission de l'Economie, Procès-verbal de la réunion du 11 mai 2017.

repair of satellites in outer space. According to its statement, these activities should be regulated by the general Space Law which was under preparation by the Service on Media and Communication at the time of the debates.[50]

The coordinated text of the Draft submitted by the Commission of Economy in May 2017[51] reacted on the Opinion of the Conseil by formulating a new paragraph which expressly exempts space communication from the scope of the Law on Space Resources. This solution entered in the final text of the Draft.[52]

II. INTERPRETATION

The operators of space resources missions will have to decide whether they will use for their satellite communication radio frequencies allocated to Luxembourg or to another country. If they would need the frequencies allocated to Luxembourg, they would have to apply for a concession regulated in Article 20 of the 1991 Electronic Media Law.[53] According to this Law, such concession may consist of elements of exclusivity, particularly for the use of certain frequency bands or certain orbital positions or for certain types of applications (Article 20(2)). The concession is personal and nontransferable. It is limited in time, but renewable, and may be withdrawn at any time under conditions defined in Article 20(4) of the 1991 Law and according to the arrangements laid down by the concession contract.

III. EVALUATION

It was never the intention of the drafters of the Law on Space Resources to regulate satellite communication. However, the expressly stated exemption of satellite communication from the scope of the Law can contribute to the transparency of the present authorization regime, along with Article 17 of the same Law which explains that other authorizations may be required. According to the 2018 Decree on the Establishment of Ministries,[54] the addressee of the application for a concession based on the 1991 Law on Electronic Media is the Ministry of State. The last question that remains to be raised is why Luxembourg satellite networks, satellite frequencies and orbital positions continue to be covered by the 1991 Electronic Media Law, the main objective of which was to regulate audiovisual media and broadcasting. It can be answered by the specific position of the principal Luxembourg satellite operator, SES, the initial business of

50. The 2020 Law on Space Activities. The Draft was finalized by the Ministry of Economy.
51. Amendements parlementaires (May 24, 2017).
52. Rapport de la commission de l'économie (July 6, 2017).
53. Roland Thurmes, "Luxembourg Administration as Notifying Administration of an International Commercial Operator," in Mahulena Hofmann, ed., *International Regulations of Space Communications* (Larcier 2013) 173-198.
54. Arrêté grand-ducal du 5 décembre 2018 portant constitution des Ministères.

which was direct to home broadcasting service; only over the years were other services such as broadband delivery, governmental services, radio navigation, and others added to complement its main activities.[55]

55. Roland Thurmes, *supra* note 53.

Article 3 Application for Authorization*

The authorization shall be granted to an operator for a mission of exploration and use of space resources for commercial purposes upon written application to the ministers.

I. DRAFTING HISTORY

As with many articles of the 2017 Law on Space Resources, this provision is inspired by the 1993 Law on the Financial Sector. Its Article 3(1) regulates the procedure for obtaining an authorization for establishment of banks or credit institutions under the jurisdiction of Luxembourg.[1] Similar legislative language appeared in a longer version in the original text of the 2016 Draft Law on Space Resources, which stated that authorization shall be granted to an operator for a mission of exploration and use of space resources for commercial purposes upon written application, following an investigation by the ministers to establish whether the conditions laid down by the present Law are fulfilled. This last part of the provision was declared as superfluous by the Conseil d'État[2] and deleted from the final text of the project.

Article 3 introduced for the first time the term "operator,"[3] which is used on numerous places later in the text of the Law (Articles 7, 8, 9, 11, 12, and 16). This term might have been inspired by the 2011 Law on Electronic Communication Networks and Services.[4] The same Article specifies that to be eligible for authorization, the mission on

---

* Mahulena Hofmann and Laetitia Zarkan

1. 1993 Law on the Financial Sector, Art. 3(1):

   > Authorization shall be granted upon written application, following an investigation by the Financial Sector Supervisory Commission to establish whether the conditions laid down by the present Law are fulfilled.

   English translation available at https://www.cssf.lu/wp-content/uploads/L_050493_lfs.pdf.

2. Avis du Conseil d'État (April 7, 2017) 11-12.
3. "Exploitant" in the French original.
4. This law uses the term "opérateur" in the French original, Loi du 27 février 2011 sur les réseaux et les services de communication électronique, replaced by the Loi du 17 décembre 2021 portant

space resources has to be pursued for commercial purposes. The provision of the 2016 Draft Law on Space Resources stating that the authorization shall be granted for a "specific period" and is renewable (former Article 5) was analogous to Article 20 of the 1991 Electronic Media Law. However, the Conseil d'État saw in the limitation of the duration of the mission a violation of Article 11, paragraph 6 of the Constitution of Luxembourg guaranteeing the freedom of commerce,[5] and a nonalignment with the 1993 Law on the Financial Sector, which does not limit the authorization granted to credit institutions. It recommended that the duration of the mission be determined by the applicant and assessed by the minister during the authorization procedure.[6] Consequently, the "specific period" provision was deleted from the text.

II. INTERPRETATION

Article 3 delimits the formal conditions of the application for an authorization to explore and use space resources. First, the form of the application is a written one, which is not surprising in view of the amount of information the applicant must submit according to further provisions of the Law. The question remains open whether the written form of the application also encompasses the possibility to submit the application electronically, at least in the future.

The term "operator" should be understood as a person who has effectively received the authorization for a space resources mission. According to the Explanatory Statement to the 2016 Draft, it is the same person as "applicant" but after the authorization procedure was successfully completed.[7] Article 5 of the 2017 Law explains that the operator can be only a legal person, not a natural one.

As mentioned in the interpretation of Article 2 of the 2017 Law, one limitation of the scope of the 2017 Law is the fact that the authorization can be accorded only for missions for "commercial purposes." Missions pursuing scientific aims and activities for purely "private purposes" are not covered; thus, the activity aimed at by the authorization must be a "business activity."[8] This has been confirmed by the representative of the Government who stated that it was not and is not in its intention to cover scientific missions under the Law.[9] The Opinion of the Conseil d'État reminds that a similar approach was chosen by the 2015 US CSLCA, which limited its scope to the commercial exploration and commercial recovery of space resources (§ 51302).[10]

transposition de la directive (UE) 2018/1972 du Parlement européen et du Conseil du 11 décembre 2018 établissant le code des communications électroniques européen, Mémorial A N° 927 du 22 décembre 2021.

5. Constitution coordonnée du Grand-Duché of Luxembourg, Mémorial A N° 23, 22 octobre 1868.
6. Avis du Conseil d'État (April 7, 2017) 13.
7. 2016 Draft Law on Space Resources, Explanatory Statement (October 12, 2016) 7.
8. *Id.* at 7.
9. Chambre des Députés, Commission de l'Economie, Procès-verbal de la réunion du 11 mai 2017, 8.
10. The 2019 UAE FLRSS covers space resources exploration or extraction activities, as well as activities for the exploitation and use of space resources for scientific, commercial, or other purposes.

The authorization is an administrative act following the corresponding administrative procedure.[11] In comparison, under the 2020 Law on Space Activities the form of the decision would be a "ministerial order" (*arrêté ministeriel*).[12] Each authorization is delivered for a specific mission related to the exploration and use space of resources. The duration of the mission is not defined by the 2017 Law, which can mean that the operator is free to determine it.

According to Article 2(1) of the 2017 Law on Space Resources, the authorization shall be granted by one or two ministers—the one responsible for the economy and another one for space activities. This provision corresponds to the drafting period of the Law during which both the Ministry of State and its Service of Communication and Media and the Ministry of Economy were responsible for space activities of Luxembourg. As explained in the Commentary on Article 2, the parliamentary elections in 2018 brought about changes in the composition of the Government and in the ministerial competences[13] and the Ministry of Economy has been charged with the authorization of space activities. At the time of writing this commentary, the double competence provision of the 2017 Law remained unchanged, but was not included in the more recent 2020 Law on Space Activities.

III. EVALUATION

Pursuant to Article VI of the OST, Luxembourg has to authorize and supervise nongovernmental entities in outer space and ensure their activities comply with the OST and international law. Ministers of the Economy and in charge of space, if not the same administration, are entitled to authorize and supervise the activities carried out by commercial entities in outer space and in the Law at hand, missions for the exploration and use of space resources. Article 3 of the 2017 Law on Space Resources provides an element of the national framework for the freedom to use and explore outer space.

The provision has to be read together with Articles 2 and 4-12 of the 2017 Law, which specify the conditions under which the authorization will be awarded. The lack of definitions of the main terms like "mission" or "operator" has been partially rectified by the 2020 Law on Space Activities, which could be used as analogy in case of lacunae. The 2020 Law on Space Activities defines the term "operator" in Article 2 as "any person who, on his own behalf, carries out or undertakes any space activity, alone or jointly with others."

In comparison, the 2015 US CSLCA gives the right to apply for the authorization of space resources to US citizens, which is further discussed in this Commentary in the part dealing with Article 4 of the 2017 Law on Space Resources. According to the 2015 US CSLCA, the procedure is limited to the "commercial" exploration and utilization of

11. Loi réglant la procédure administrative non contentieuse, Mémorial A N° 87, 27 décembre 1978; Règlement grand-ducal relatif à la procédure à suivre par les administrations relevant de l'État et des communes, Mémorial A N° 54, 6 juillet 1979.
12. 2020 Law on Space Activities, Art. 5(3).
13. Arrêté grand-ducal du 5 décembre 2018 portant constitution des Ministères.

space resources. The detailed formulation of the procedural part of the authorization procedure was postponed to the later period.[14]

Additionally, the 2019 UAE FLRSS shifted the formulation of the terms and conditions relating to the authorization of space resources activities to a later Decision to be issued by the Council of Ministers.[15] On the other hand, the 2021 Japan Space Resources Law,[16] which made a government permit to pursue space resources activity a condition of its legality, formulated the conditions and procedures for obtaining an authorization—i.e., an activity plan, its compliance with the Japanese general Space Activity Act[17]—directly in the body of the Law.

14. 2015 US CSLCA, § 51302.
15. 2019 UAE FLRSS, Art. 18.
16. Tajiro Suzuki, "Japan: Legal Issues in Space Business in Japan—Volume 2," Baker Mackenzie (July 9, 2021).
17. Japan, Act on Launching of Spacecraft, and Control of Spacecraft, Act No. 76 of 2016.

Article 4 Forms of Companies*

The authorization for a mission shall only be granted if the applicant is a public company limited by shares (société anonyme) or a corporate partnership limited by shares (société en commandite par actions) or a private limited liability company (société à responsabilité limitée) of Luxembourg law or a European Company (société européenne) having its registered office in Luxembourg.

I. DRAFTING HISTORY

Initially, only Luxembourg legal entities were mentioned in Article 4 of the 2016 Draft Law on Space Resources. The lawmakers had also chosen only two forms of companies eligible for the authorization procedure: public company limited by shares (*société anonyme*) or a corporate partnership limited by shares (*société en commandite par actions*).[1] In this approach, the 2016 Draft was more restrictive than the 1993 Law on the Financial Sector,[2] which was used as an inspiration for the Draft of Article 4. The 1993 Law also allows applications from public-law institutions and cooperative societies. Such a restrictive approach applied to space activities was criticized by both the Chamber of Commerce and the Conseil d'État,[3] which admitted the importance of limiting the forms of companies for the establishment of credit institutions, due to the existence of European directives in this area; but, it contested the relevance for space-related private entities.

Thereafter, the Commission of Economy followed the opinion of the Conseil d'État and suggested that private limited companies under Luxembourgish law and European Companies registered in Luxembourg could also submit a request for an

---

* Mahulena Hofmann and Laetitia Zarkan

1. 2016 Draft Law on Space Resources, p. 9.
2. 1993 Law on the Financial Sector, Art. 4:

> Authorization may only be granted to a legal person incorporated under Luxembourg law which is established in the form of a public-law institution, a société anonyme (public limited company), a société en commandite par actions (limited partnership with a share capital) or a société coopérative (cooperative society).

3. Avis de la Chambre de Commerce, p. 3; Avis du Conseil d'État, p. 9-10.

authorization to carry out missions related to the exploration and utilization of space resources.[4]

II. INTERPRETATION

Article 4 of the 2017 Law on Space Resources enumerates the corporate forms of companies eligible to apply for authorization of missions in space resources activities in Luxembourg. The applicant must be either a public company limited by shares (*société anonyme*), a corporate partnership limited by shares (*société en commandite par actions*) or a private limited liability company (*société à responsabilité limitée*). Furthermore, individuals are clearly excluded from the scope of the Law and only companies of Luxembourg law or a European Company (*société européenne*) having its registered office in Luxembourg can apply for authorization.

The consequence of the registration in Luxembourg is the fact that such company will be subject of Luxembourg law. The conditions for having a registered office in Luxembourg are regulated by Article 2 of Law of August 10, 1915 on Commercial Companies[5] as modified by the Law of May 31, 1999 Governing the Domiciliation of Companies.[6] In case the domicile of a company is located in the Grand Duchy of Luxembourg, it is of Luxembourg nationality and Luxembourg law is fully applicable to it. According to the Law of August 25, 2006[7] which introduced new measures amending the Luxembourg company law, any company whose central administration (head office) is in the Grand Duchy of Luxembourg shall be subject to Luxembourg law, even though the constitutive instrument may have been executed in a foreign jurisdiction.

III. EVALUATION

By providing an exhaustive list of types of companies and requiring to be established on the Luxembourg territory, the authors of the Draft Law made sure that Luxembourg was able to supervise and efficiently monitor their activities while being able to check the honorability and financial soundness of the operators.

Surprisingly, no definition of the legal form of the entity eligible to apply for authorization of a space activity can be found in the later, 2020 Law on Space Activities of Luxembourg. The conditions of the registered office and central administration, as well as the formulation of the conditions for authorization, however, signal that only legal persons can be involved in the authorization procedure.

4. Amendements parlementaires, May 24, 2017.
5. Loi concernant les sociétés commerciales, Mémorial A N° 90, 30 octobre 1915. The head office of any commercial company is located at the place of central management of the company. The place of central management is deemed to be the head office until proved otherwise.
6. Loi du 31 mai 1999 régissant la domiciliation des sociétés et - modifiant et complétant certaines dispositions de la loi modifiée du 10 août 1915 concernant les sociétés commerciales; Mémorial A 1999, N° 77, 21 juin 1999.
7. Mémorial A 2006, N° 152, August 31, 2006.

The 2015 US CSLCA does not provide a limitation on the forms of companies that may apply for authorization. Section 51301 of Chapter 513 of the 2015 US CSLCA specifically refers to the "US citizens," as understood in section 50902, who engage in space resource activities. According to this definition, US citizens are natural persons with US citizenship and legal entities directly submitted to US law. Further, if they are entities "organized or existing under the laws of a foreign country," they are eligible to benefit from the applicability of the Act provided that a "controlling interest" of the entity is held by US citizens—natural or legal persons. An interest of 51% is presumed sufficient.[8]

Pursuant to Article 3 of the 2019 UAE FLRSS, the Law applies to space activities carried out "by persons who hold the nationality of the State, or companies that have a headquarters in the State."[9] According to the available information concerning the recent 2021 Space Resources Law of Japan, the applicant is a not clearly defined "person."[10]

8. *See* 14 C.F.R. 401.5.
9. 2015 US CSLCA, § 50902; 2019 UAE FLRSS, Art. 3(2).
10. Tajiro Suzuki, "Japan: Legal Issues in Space Business in Japan—Volume 2," Baker Mackenzie (July 9, 2021).

Article 5 Nonassignability of Authorization*

The authorization is personal and non-assignable.

I. DRAFTING HISTORY

The original version of Article 5[1] was composed of three paragraphs. First, it stated that the object of the authorization is limited to the mission it covers. Second, it included a rule that declared that the authorization was granted for a limited period of time and could be renewed. Third, it stated that the authorization is personal and nonassignable.

The Explanatory Statement to the Draft[2] explained that the authorization was granted to an operator, but not in a generic way like it is the case for a business license—it is granted for a specific and determined mission. The Statement also explained that the authorization should be for a limited duration: "It was deemed useful to limit the authorization in time, as space missions, even if they are long missions, are not meant to go on indefinitely."[3] This is was also in line with the 1991 Electronic Media Law, which declares that the concession or permit is granted for a limited period, but it is renewable.[4] Concerning the third rule, the document explained that the authorization should be strictly personal, it is granted on an *intuitu personae* basis and any transmission, cession, lease, or any other transfer or transmission of the authorization are formally prohibited.

In its Opinion to the Draft, the Chamber of Commerce proposed that the maximum time limit of the mission should be mentioned in the Law.[5] Similarly, the Conseil d'État concluded that the provision stating that the authorization is granted for a limited period is fully superfluous especially if no minimal or maximal duration of the mission are indicated. Such lack of indication values to "a restriction to freedom of

---

* Mahulena Hofmann and Laetitia Zarkan
1. 2016 Draft Law on Space Resources, Art. 5.
2. *Id.*
3. *Id.* at p. 8.
4. 1991 Electronic Media Law, Art. 3(3).
5. Avis de la Chambre de Commerce (January 10, 2017).

commerce" protected by Article 11, paragraph 6 of the Constitution[6] and is not aligned with the 1993 Law on the Financial Sector, which does not limit the authorization granted to credit institutions. According to the Conseil, also the rule limiting the authorization to the specific mission can be deleted from the text of the Draft, as it had been already covered by Article 3 and need not to be repeated.

The Commission of Economy found it difficult to define the minimal and maximal duration of a mission in a document of a general character,[7] and suggested to follow the Opinion of the Conseil to limit the Article to the rule prohibiting the transmission or transfer of the authorization. This reduced provision became part of the final Draft. In its Report, the Commission on Economy underlined the position of the Conseil, which stated that it is the role of the operator to propose the duration of the envisaged mission in its application for authorization and the competence of the minister to evaluate it.[8]

II. INTERPRETATION

Article 5 of the 2017 Law on Space Resources makes the authorization personal, meaning *intuitu personae*, so it is only granted to the operator and strictly related to it.[9] Any transmission, cession, lease or any other transfer or transmission of the authorization of a commercial space resources mission are not allowed.

This is interesting in comparison with the 2020 general Law on Space Activities of Luxembourg, which includes provisions specifically devoted to the transfer of space activities. Under the 2020 Law, it is possible after authorization by the competent minister, following a joint application of both transferor and transferee operators. In cases in which the transferee operator is not established in Luxembourg, this authorization is conditioned by a bilateral agreement with the State of which the transferee is national that guarantees the Luxembourg State against any recourse brought against it on account of its international liability or for compensation for loss or damage.[10] The Commentary on the first Draft of the 2020 Law[11] explains that despite of the fact that authorization of space activities is personal and nonassignable, it is logical to submit a transfer of the authorized activities to an authorization procedure, as recommended by paragraph 8 of UN General Assembly Resolution 68/74 of December 11, 2013.[12] For more details, *see* the section of this commentary devoted to Article 12 of the 2020 Law on Space Activities.

6. Constitution coordonnée du Grand-Duché de Luxembourg, Mémorial A N° 23, 22 octobre 1868.
7. P.V. ECO 23, p. 10.
8. Chambre des Députés, Rapport de la Commission de l'Economie (July 6, 2017) 10.
9. *Id.* at 8.
10. 2020 Law on Space Activities, Art. 12.
11. 2018 Draft Law on Space Activities.
12. UNGA Res. 68/74: Recommendation on national legislation relevant to the peaceful exploration and use of outer space (December 11, 2013).

III. EVALUATION

The rule that the authorization is personal and nonassignable corresponds to the principle of the 1993 Law on the Financial Sector that no person may be authorized to carry on the business of a credit institution either through another person or as an intermediary for the carrying-on of such business (Article 2, paragraph 2). A similar wording can be found in the 1991 Electronic Media Law declaring that "the concession or permit is personal and non-transferable" (Article 3(4)).

There is an open question as to how an operator should proceed if it wishes to or must cease an authorized mission—whether for financial, personal, technical or other reasons—and transfer the activity to a third person. Possibly, Article 12 of the 2020 Law on Space Activities, which formulates conditions for a transfer of space activity, can be applied *per analogiam* to such a situation. However, Article 1 of the 2020 Law exempts missions involving the exploration and use of space resources from its scope and seems relatively rigorous in its future application.

Therefore, it seems that in such situation, Article 9 of the 2017 Law on Space Resources will be applicable and obliges the members of the management body to notify to the ministers of any change regarding the substantial information on which the application for authorization was based. The cessation of the mission can be considered as an object of such substantial information. The consequence of such step can be the application of Article 14 of the 2017 Law on Space Resources. Under this provision, if the conditions of authorization (i.e., the implementation of the mission) are no longer met, the authorization would be withdrawn by the minister. The new entity would have to apply for a new authorization of the mission in accordance with the 2017 Law on Space Resources.

To compare, the US can decide to grant an authorization to US space companies that are willing to conduct commercial activities in outer space.[13] However, there is no further indication with regard to the personal and nonassignable nature of the authorization. In the 2019 UAE FLRSS, the permit granted can be assigned to "others" upon authorization "issued by the Council of Ministers or whomever it delegates."[14] The 2019 UAE FLRSS provides for the possibilities to assign the permit to others, as long as they meet "the terms and conditions prescribed for its granting."[15]

13. 2015 US CSLCA, § 51302(b).
14. 2019 UAE FLRSS, Art. 14.
15. *Id.*

Article 6 Useful Information*

The application for authorization must be accompanied by all such information as may be useful for the assessment thereof, as well as by a mission program.

I. DRAFTING HISTORY

The text of Article 6 remained unchanged from its submission in the 2016 Draft Law on Space Resources. It is based on Article 3(4) of the 1993 Law on the Financial Sector with the difference that the word "useful" replaces the word "necessary" with regard to the information to be provided.[1] According to the 2016 Commentary on Articles,[2] the scope of Article 6 is broader in that it requires the applicant to communicate "all relevant information" and not only information that is "necessary," as set forth in the 1993 Law on Financial Sector.

Concerning the necessity to submit a "mission program," the parliamentary Commission on Economy rightly observed that this term remains undefined in the Law.[3] According to the Commission, to prepare their applications, future operators would welcome an exhaustive list of the required components of the program.

The Conseil d'État criticized the deviation of the formulation of Article 6 from its model in the 1993 Law on Financial Sector. First, it contemplated about the replacement of the word "necessary" by the word "useful" in the wording of Article 6. Second, it reminded of the fact that the 1993 Law requires the applicants wishing to carry on the business of a credit institution to submit a "program of operation" indicating the type and volume of business envisaged. The Conseil suggested that the requirements on the space resources mission program are formulated analogously. The mission

* Mahulena Hofmann and Laetitia Zarkan

1. 1993 Law on the Financial Sector, Art. 3(4):

> The application for authorization must be accompanied by all such information necessary for the assessment thereof and by a programme of operations indicating the type and volume of business envisaged.

2. 2016 Draft Law on Space Resources, p. 8.
3. Avis de la Chambre de Commerce (January 10, 2017) 3.

program can indicate the "part or region of outer space or the identification of the celestial body where the mission will be carried out" as well as the "technical means used to realize the mission."

The Commission of Economy discussed these suggestions. However, the representative of the Ministry of Economy proposed not to follow the Opinion of the Conseil in these points with following explications. The term "useful" information incorporated in the Draft seems to be wiser (*plus judicieux*) than the term "necessary" related to the information required from the applicant. The precision of the mission program as proposed by the Conseil, defining the geographical scope of the mission or the technical means used to realize the mission would unnecessarily burden the provision (*surchargeraient sans nécessité cette disposition*).[4] Consequently, the Draft provision was not changed from the 2016 Draft to the final adopted version of the Law.[5]

II. INTERPRETATION

Article 6 of the 2017 Law on Space Resources is composed of two connected parts. First, it requires from the applicant for authorization of a commercial space resources mission all information useful for the assessment of the application. The question is what this information is and who decides whether it is complete (all information) and useful (useful information). These questions remain unanswered both by the text of the 2017 Law on Space Resources and its accompanying Commentary of Articles.[6]

At the moment, it is the future operator who must speculate as to what information is needed and what a mission program means. Whereas it is clear that the final authority deciding on the completeness of the information will be the authorizing Ministry, the content of the "useful" information and the "program mission" are not. Fortunately, a certain idea about the spirit of this provision can be derived from the later 2020 Law on Space Activities of Luxembourg. Similar to the 2017 Law on Space Resources, the 2020 Law requires from the applicants for space activities under the jurisdiction of Luxembourg "all useful information for the assessment" of the application, as well as an "activity program."[7] These terms also remain undefined in the body of the Law. However, Article 7 of the 2020 Law on Space Activities states that "the standard content of an application for authorization may be established by a Grand-Ducal regulation." It seems that the same procedure could be applied in relation to the 2017 Law on Space Resources and the applicants could be given a lead on the scope and content of the "useful" information and the "mission program" in the future.

III. EVALUATION

By not detailing the content of the mission program or of the information to provide in the 2017 Law on Space Resources, two scenarios are possible. Either information on

4. Chambre des Députés, Commission de l'Economie, Procès-verbal de la réunion du 11 mai 2017.
5. Chambre des Députés, Rapport de la Commission de l'Economie (July 6, 2017).
6. Chambre des Députés, Rapport de la Commission de l'Economie (July 6, 2017) 5 ff.
7. 2020 Law on Space Activities, Art. 7.

the application and mission program will be adapted to each operator as there is not yet a one-size-fits-all document that contains standard information for companies carrying out exploration or use of space resources activities. Or the scope of information and the features of the mission program will be defined in depth in a sub-statutory regulation. The decision between the two is a political one, and the future operators would surely welcome a guidance on which information they are supposed to submit in addition to information defined in Articles 7-11 of the 2017 Law. A more detailed regulation would also strengthen the legal security so frequently required in other connotations by the Conseil d'État.

To compare, the 2015 US CSLCA does not require any specific information from the operators on their space resources missions as there is no detailed authorization procedure adopted for such missions yet. The 2019 UAE FLRSS shifted the details of the authorization procedure to the Decision issued by the Council of Ministers or "whomever it delegates."[8]

The available information on the 2020 Japan Space Resources Law[9] indicates that the applicants have first to comply with the general requirements of the Space Activity Act.[10] Additionally, they are required to submit an activity plan including the purpose of the proposed space resources exploration and exploitation activity; the term, the location, the method and other details of the activity, and other matters as required under the relevant regulations (which have not yet been published). The government will review the activity plan and consider whether it complies with the earlier Space Activity Act of Japan, will not breach space-related treaties, will not harm national security, and whether the person that proposes to undertake the activity has sufficient capacity to do so.

8. 2019 UAE FLRSS, Art. 18.
9. Tajiro Suzuki, "Japan: Legal Issues in Space Business in Japan—Volume 2," Baker Mackenzie (July 9, 2021).
10. Japan, Act on Launching of Spacecraft, and Control of Spacecraft (Act No. 76 of 2016).

Article 7 Organizational Structure*

(1) The authorization shall be subject to the production of evidence showing the existence in Luxembourg of the central administration and of the registered office, including the administrative and accounting structures of the operator to be authorized.
(2) The operator to be authorized shall have a robust scheme of financial, technical and statutory procedures and arrangements through which the exploration and utilization mission, including the commercialisation of space resources are planned and implemented. The operator to be authorized shall furthermore have a robust internal governance scheme, which includes in particular a clear organisational structure with well-defined, transparent and consistent lines of responsibility, effective processes to identify, manage, monitor and report the risks it is or might be exposed to, and adequate internal control mechanisms, including sound administrative and accounting procedures, as well as control and security arrangements for its technical systems and applications.
(3) The arrangements, processes, procedures and mechanisms referred to in this article shall be comprehensive[1] and proportionate to the nature, scale and complexity of the risks inherent to the business model of the operator to be authorized as well as to the mission for which the authorization is sought.

I. DRAFTING HISTORY

The text of Article 7 appeared for the first time in the 2016 Draft Law on Space Resources. It has been modeled closely to Articles 5(1)[2] and (1*bis*) and 3[3] of the 1993 Law on Financial Sector. One modification of this provision has been included on

* Mahulena Hofmann
1. In French: *exhaustifs*.
2. 1993 Law on the Financial Sector, Art. 5(1):

> Authorization shall be subject to the production of evidence showing the existence in Luxembourg of the central administration and of the registered office of the institution in respect of which authorization is sought.

3. *Id.* at Art. 5(3):

the initiative of the Conseil d'État who proposed to replace the original term "applicant" in paragraph 2 of Article 7 with the "operator to be authorized."[4] Another suggestion of the Conseil d'État dealt with the rules on internal control and sound accounting procedures, which—in the original version—reflected the situation in credit institutions. According to its opinion, the Article should better accentuate procedures needed for space resources missions and their commercialization.[5] This idea became a part of the later text.[6]

II. INTERPRETATION

Article 7 formulates another group of conditions necessary to fulfill to obtain a successful authorization.

The first group of conditions deals with the central administration of the company. According to the 1915 Law on Commercial Companies,[7] the domicile of a commercial company is located at the seat of its central administration (head office). Until evidence to the contrary is brought, the central administration of a company is deemed to coincide with the place where the registered office is located (Article 2). Article 7 of the 2017 Law on Space Resources allows for, under a legal and refutable condition, verification of whether the condition of the existence of the central administration and the statutory seat of the applicant and later operator is fulfilled.[8]

The second group of conditions deals with the internal structure of the company. It requires the operator to have a robust scheme of financial, technical, and statutory procedures; robust internal governance scheme; well-defined lines of responsibility; effective processes to manage risk; adequate internal control mechanisms; security arrangements for its technical systems and applications; and accounting procedures. As explained above, the majority of the terms is taken from the 1993 Law on the Financial Sector and can be interpreted analogously. To give more detail is difficult. The parliamentary discussions in the Commission of Economy referred to a legal study that was not directed to the public and delivered only to the members of the commission.[9] All that is known of this report is that, according to the Commentary to the final text of the Draft, "security arrangements for its technical systems and applications" means not only information systems but everything that is connected with mechanisms and methods of security.[10]

> The internal governance arrangements, processes, procedures and mechanisms referred to in this Article shall be comprehensive and proportionate to the nature, scale and complexity of the risks inherent in the business model and the credit institution's activities.

4. Avis du Conseil d'État (April 7, 2017) 14.
5. *Id.*
6. Chambre des Députés, Rapport de la Commission de l'Economie (July 6, 2017).
7. Law of August 10, 1915 on Commercial Companies, as consolidated by the Regulation of December 5, 2017.
8. 2016 Draft Law on Space Resources, p. 9.
9. P.V.ECO 24, p. 2.
10. In French: *technique*.

Article 7(3) explains that these conditions are exhaustive ("comprehensive" in the text of the translation), meaning that no additional conditions can be raised concerning the central administration and internal procedures during the authorization procedure. Furthermore, this part of Article 7 incorporates the principle of proportionality, which is already partly included in Article 7(2) dealing with "adequate" internal control mechanisms. All measures should be proportionate to the complexity of the risks inherent to the business model of the operator to be authorized, as well as to the mission for which the authorization is sought. The authority to decide whether this particular condition was fulfilled will be the Ministry of Economy during the authorization procedure.

III. EVALUATION

Other laws regulating space resources activities—the 2015 US CSLCA, the 2019 UAE FLRSS, or the Space Resources Law of Japan—do not include any details dealing with the seat or the organizational structure of the company applying for space resources application.

Similar conditions to those in the 2017 Law on Space Resources for pursuing space activities are part of Article 6 of the 2020 Law on Space Activities. It has been largely harmonized with the 2017 Law and will be addressed in detail in the Part devoted to the 2020 Law on Space Activities.

Article 8 Shareholders*

(1) The authorization shall be subject to the communication to the ministers of the identity of the shareholders or members, whether direct or indirect, natural or legal persons, that have direct or indirect holdings of at least 10 per cent of the capital or of the voting rights in the operator, and of the amount of such holdings or, if such 10 per cent threshold is not met, the identity of the twenty largest shareholders or members.
The authorization shall be refused if, taking into account the need to ensure a sound and prudent operation, the suitability of those shareholders or members is not satisfactory.

(2) The concept of sound and prudent operation is assessed in accordance with the following criteria:
   a) the good (professional) repute of the operator to be authorized and the shareholders and members referred to in paragraph 1;
   b) the good repute, knowledge, skills and experience of any member of the management body of the shareholders or members referred to in paragraph 1;
   c) the financial soundness of the shareholders and members referred to in paragraph 1;
   d) whether there are reasonable grounds to suspect that money laundering or terrorist financing is being or has been committed or attempted in relation to the proposed exploration mission or the proposed utilization of space resources or that such exploration mission or such utilization could increase the risk thereof.

The good repute of the members of the management body of the shareholders or members referred to in paragraph 1 shall be assessed in accordance with the terms of article 9, paragraph 1, second sentence.

* Mahulena Hofmann

I. DRAFTING HISTORY

The original text of Article 8 was inspired by Articles 6(1)[1] and 9[2] of the 1993 Law on the Financial Sector. However, the text does not transpose all rules applicable to financial sector to the regulation of space resources activities. As an example, the 2016 Commentary on Articles mentions the missing provision dealing with the supervision of groups to which the applicants belong, with following comment: "This does not mean, however, that the group structure would be irrelevant for the assessment of the application; the opposite is the case given that the reputation is not only assessed in respect to the applicant, but also in respect to the group, pursuant to Article 8(2), first indent of this Draft Law.[3] The shareholder structure shall in all cases be transparent."[4] To be precise, the provision on the assessment of the reputation of the group to which the applicant belongs was later deleted on the basis of the Opinion of the Conseil d'État[5] from the text.

The Chamber of Commerce discussed the scope of the requirement to possess knowledge, skills and experience, and whether it should be required from all shareholders or members of the operator, or only the management body of the shareholders? In its Opinion,[6] the Chamber opted for limiting this condition to the members of the managing body; because of their different role, the shareholders do not necessarily need to possess the knowledge, experience, and competence necessary for operating a space resources mission.[7]

Concerning the definition of qualified holding of the capital of the operator applying for authorization, the Conseil d'État proposed to replace the reference to the 1993 Law of the Financial Sector in the original Draft with the definition: qualified holding should represent at least 10% of the capital or of the voting rights in the operator.[8] In its Opinion, it raised also the question whether the requirement of sound

1. 1993 Law on the Financial Sector, Art. 6(1):

> Authorization shall be subject to communication to the CSSF of the identities of shareholders or members, whether direct or indirect and whether natural or legal persons, whose holdings in the institution to be authorized are qualifying holdings or are such as to enable them to exercise a significant influence on the conduct of its business, and of the amounts of such holdings. The suitability of those shareholders or members must be satisfactory, having regard to the need to ensure that the credit institution is managed in a sound and prudent manner.

2. *Id.* at Art. 9:

> Authorization shall be conditional on the production of evidence showing the existence of an adequate credit standing commensurate with the program of operations.

3. 2016 Draft Law on Space Resources, p. 8. The original text required that the condition of sound and prudent exploitation is assessed not only on behalf of the applying operator but also the "group to which it belongs."
4. *Id.* at p. 9.
5. Avis du Conseil d'État (April 7, 2017) 14.
6. Avis de la Chambre de Commerce (January 10, 2017).
7. *Id.* at p. 4.
8. Avis du Conseil d'État (April 7, 2017) 14.

and prudent operation transferred from the financial sector is well suited to space resource missions. As an example, it stated that it is difficult to require the fulfillment of honorability from the "group" to which the operator belongs. A "group" does not possess legal personality and as such cannot bear any professional honorability. Furthermore, in line with the position of the Chamber of Commerce, it seems to be too much to require good repute, knowledge, skills and experience from any member of the management body of the shareholders. In the Opinion of the Conseil d'État, the investors may have no relation to the world of the exploitation and exploration of space resources and may be active in completely different sectors. The Council proposed to delete this legal condition.

This question of the proof of good repute of all members of the management body of the shareholders or members of the operators was discussed also in the parliamentary Commission of Economy.[9] The outcome of these debates was maintaining this condition in the Draft, contrary to the opinion of the Conseil d'État. The main reason for this was explained in the debates. By keeping this condition, the Ministry of Economy wished to prevent an entry of "certain funds or big investors" in the missions on space resources who are known for being "less credible."[10]

On the other hand, the recommendation of the Conseil d'État to delete the assessment of the honorability of the "group" the operator is belonging was reflected in the final Draft.[11]

II. INTERPRETATION

What is required by this Article? First, the applicant for an authorization for a commercial mission on space resources must inform the minister about the identity of the shareholders or members, that have direct or indirect holdings of at least 10% of the capital or of the voting rights and of the amount of such holdings. If such 10% threshold is not met, the identity of the 20 largest shareholders or members has to be revealed. The purpose of this exercise is to judge the "suitability" of those shareholders or members in view of the sound and prudent operation of the mission; if this is judged as "nonsatisfactory," the authorization shall be refused by the minister.

Second, the applicant and the major shareholders and members have to prove their good repute. This shall be assessed in accordance with the terms of Article 9 of the 2017 Law, which indicates that it will be assessed on the basis of police records and other evidence showing that the persons concerned are offering a guarantee of a irreproachable conduct.[12]

Third, all members of the management body of the major shareholders or members have to demonstrate their good repute, but additionally also their knowledge, skills and experience. The conditions for demonstrating "knowledge, skills and experience" are also defined in Article 9 and will be commented in detail there. They

9. P.V.ECO 24, p. 3.
10. "Peu sérieux." *Id.* at p. 3.
11. Chambre des Députés, Rapport de la Commission de l'Economie (July 6, 2017).
12. 2016 Draft Law on Space Resources, p. 8.

include the fact that these persons have previously carried out similar activities, specifically in connection with outer space, or in a relation to a related sector such as the satellite, telecommunication, mining, or the information technology sector.[13] The procedure of compliance with the criteria has been formulated as a *nihil obstat* procedure on the part of the ministers in charge of issuing approvals.[14]

Fourth, the major shareholders and members referred to in the paragraph have to demonstrate their financial soundness. This will be assessed on the basis of Article 10 of the 2017 Law and is not based on any numerical requirement but a complex of aspects demonstrating the financial stability of the operator.

Fifth, it will be assessed whether there are reasonable grounds to suspect that money laundering or terrorist financing is being or has been committed or attempted in relation to the proposed exploration mission or the proposed utilization of space resources. This rule has its origin in the 1993 Law on the Financial Sector and the 2004 Law on Professional Obligations of the Financial Sector as regards Combating Money Laundering and the Financing of Terrorism[15] transposing Directive 2001/97/EC of the European Parliament and of the Council of December 4, 2001 amending Council Directive 91/308/EEC on prevention of the use of the financial system for the purpose of money laundering.

III. EVALUATION

The Article formulates the criteria which have to be fulfilled by the defined shareholders or members of a company asking for authorization of a commercial space resources mission. They have been formulated using the experience of Luxembourg authorities with the authorization of credit institutions. As there is no jurisprudence on the space resources authorization at this time, the experience from the financial sector can be used as an analogy. At this moment, it is difficult to predict how the conditions to be fulfilled by credit institution will influence the landscape of space resources missions in Luxembourg.

Similar conditions have been included in the 2020 Law on Space Activities. The 2020 Law differentiates between the obligations of the "operator to be authorized," the "members of the operator governing body," and the "shareholders." The details will be commented in the part devoted to the 2020 Law.

To compare, other laws dealing with space resource missions—the 2015 US CSLCA, the 2019 UAE FLRSS, and the 2021 Japan Space Resources Law—do not entail comparable provisions.

13. *Id.* at p. 9.
14. *Id.*
15. Mémorial A N° 183 (November 19, 2004).

Article 9 Good Repute*

(1) The authorization shall be subject to the condition that the members of the management body of the operator shall at all times be of sufficiently good repute and possess sufficient knowledge, skills and experience to perform their duties. Such good repute shall be assessed on the basis of police records and of any evidence tending to show that the persons concerned are of good repute and offer every guarantee of irreproachable conduct.

(2) At least two persons must be responsible for the management of the operator. Those persons must be empowered to effectively determine the direction taken by the business. They must possess adequate professional experience by virtue of their having previously carried out similar activities at a high level of responsibility and autonomy in the space industry or in a related sector.

(3) Any change in the persons referred to in paragraph 1 shall be communicated in advance to the ministers. The ministers may request all such information as may be necessary regarding the persons who may be required to fulfil the legal requirements with respect to good repute and professional experience. The ministers shall refuse the proposed change if these persons are not of adequate professional repute or do not have sufficient professional experience or where there are objective and demonstrable grounds for believing that the proposed change would pose a threat to the sound and prudent management of the operation.

(4) Granting the authorization implies that the members of the management body shall, on their own initiative, notify in writing and in a complete, coherent and comprehensive form, to the ministers any change regarding the substantial information on which the ministers based their investigation of the application for the authorization.

* Laetitia Zarkan and P.J. Blount

I. DRAFTING HISTORY

Article 9 of the 2017 Law on Space Resources was drafted as the framework for the conditions that members of the management body of a company exploiting space resources must meet to show they are honorable and have relevant professional experience. It sets out the manner in which these criteria are to be assessed based on Article 7 of the 1993 Law on the Financial Sector.[1] Such criteria are the exercise of prior analogous activities specifically in relation to the space sector or in relation to a related sector, such as satellites, telecommunications, mining or information technology.[2] The procedure of compliance with the criteria has been formulated as a *nihil obstat* procedure on the part of the ministers in charge of issuing approvals, the same as for the compliance of the major shareholders with the conditions formulated in Article 8.[3] Contrary to Article 7(3), third sentence of the 1993 Law on the Financial Sector, the Draft of Article 9 did not include any specific appeal for reversal against decisions of the ministers.[4]

In its opinion, the Chamber of Commerce proposed to delete the criterion of the good repute of the shareholders and associates from Article 8 and to integrate this requirement in Article 9 paragraph 1 of the Draft so it makes a coherent set of requirements for the members of the management body of the operator, the shareholders and associates.[5] This proposal was not reflected in the final text of the Draft.

On this place, the Conseil d'État found it opportune to address the question of an appeal to the administrative court for review, considering that the time limit for lodging an appeal for reversal should be that of ordinary law (deadline: three months from the moment of the notification to the addressee) and not the one-month time limit provided for in the 1993 Law on the Financial Sector (Article 7(3)). In addition, the Conseil d'État

1. 1993 Law on the Financial Sector, Art. 7:

   (1) Authorization shall be conditional on the production by the members of the bodies performing administrative, management and supervisory functions, and by the shareholders or members referred to in the preceding article, of evidence of their professional standing. Such standing shall be assessed on the basis of police records and of any evidence tending to show that the persons concerned are of good repute and offering every guarantee of irreproachable conduct on the part of those persons.
   (2) At least two persons must be responsible for the management of the institution. Those persons must be empowered effectively to determine the direction taken by the business and must possess adequate professional experience by virtue of their having previously carried on similar activities at a high level of responsibility and autonomy.
   (3) Any change in the persons required to fulfil the legal conditions of professional standing and experience must be authorized in advance by the CSSF. To that end, the CSSF may request all such information as may be necessary regarding the persons who may be required to fulfil the legal conditions. An appeal against the decision of the CSSF may be lodged within one month, and may be struck out if it is not so lodged, before the administrative court, which shall determine the matter ... as a court adjudicating on the substance.

2. 2016 Draft Law on Space Resources, p. 9.
3. *Id.*
4. *Id.* and 1993 Law on the Financial Sector, Art. 7.
5. Avis de la Chambre de Commerce (January 10, 2017) 4.

also proposed to add the following sentence: "The Minister's decision may be referred to the administrative court, which shall rule as the judge of the merits."[6]

The Commission of Economy discussed these proposals[7] and noted that no changes to Article 9 were necessary. Together with the representatives of the Ministry of Economy, it opposed to the Conseil d'État proposition to include in the text of the Draft the possibility of an appeal for reversal to the Administrative Court, considering that a simple appeal for annulment, allowed ex officio, to be sufficient for these more delicate decisions.[8]

II. INTERPRETATION

This Article sets the professional criteria of the members of the management body of the operator. These criteria address the reputation, knowledge, skills, and experience of the members of the management team for the space operations.

Article 9(1) lays out the requirement that the members of the management body maintain a good reputation and have the "knowledge, skills, and experience to perform their duties."

The article does not give the specifics how these should be assessed, but it does state that police records and any other evidence that bears on the good reputation of the individuals can be used in this assessment. Interestingly, the sentence on assessment seems to be targeted at determining the good reputation rather than on the "knowledge, skills, and experience" of the individuals. The phrase "knowledge, skills, and experience," would seemingly indicate that there should be an assessment of these individuals' ability to manage a space operation. However, there is no indication of how such "knowledge, skills, and experience" would be assessed, and whether such assessment would take into account technical or purely managerial aspects. The Commentary to the 2016 Draft gives only an indication that the persons should have previously carried out similar activities, specifically connected with outer space, or in relation to a related sector such as the satellite, the telecommunications, the mining, or the information technology sector.

Article 9(2) requires that at least two individuals be responsible for the management of the operator. These individuals must have a leadership role in the organization that allows them to control the direction of the operations. These persons must have previous experience in a similar role in the space industry or related sector. To some extent, this clause addresses the idea of "knowledge, skills, and experience" from the preceding clause, but may place a high burden on newer companies or start-ups that may not have persons that have held previous, similar roles in the industry as part of their leadership team. At the same time, it is a way for Luxembourg to mitigate the risks that may arise from the lack of experience of individuals who would create a company without skills or prior experience and knowledge. An unclear situation may occur in

6. Avis du Conseil d'État (April 7, 2017) 12.
7. Chambre des Députés, Commission de l'Economie, Procès-verbal de la réunion du 18 mai 2017 (May 18, 2017) 4.
8. Chambre des Députés, Rapport de la Commission de l'Economie (July 6, 2017) 3.

case that one of the two individuals would be unable for a limited period (i.e., for illness) to effectively determine the direction taken by the business—does it mean that the conditions of the authorization are not any more fulfilled and, in accordance with Article 14 of the 2017 Law, the authorization must be withdrawn, or does the minister dispose by an implicit margin of appreciation?

Article 9(3) creates an obligation to notify the authorizing ministers if these individuals are changed. The ministers may request the same similar documentation to establish the good repute, knowledge, skills, and experience of the persons proposed for these roles. The ministers may reject the change if it is not satisfied that the proposed individual meets the minimum standards, which are not articulated in the Law. As in the previous case of a temporary inability to control the operations, it is unclear, what the case would be if the minister in charge would reject the proposed individual and no alternate is available. Presumably, also this situation could trigger the revocation of the authorization under Article 14.

Article 9(4) creates an additional notification requirement for members of the management body to update the authorizing Ministry in cases where there have been substantive changes in the information on which the Ministry based its investigation of the application for authorization. This clause requires the organization to show due diligence in monitoring that the individuals on the management body still maintain the good repute, knowledge, skills, and experience required by Article 9(1), it but can have also a broader scope requiring the authorized operator to inform about all substantive changes concerning the mission. To decide which change regards the substantial information remains *prima facie* by the management body but can be contested by the ministers.

II. EVALUATION

The text of Article 9 of the 2017 Law on Space Resources is transposed from the 1993 Law on the Financial Sector. In general, this Law focuses much more on reputational matters of individuals than other comparative authorization laws.

For instance, while the US did not articulate a specific process for authorization of space resource missions, it is likely that any regulations would be similar to other US licensing regimes that have rigorous technical details of missions that need to be provided such as the Federal Communications Commission's regulations on space debris mitigation.[9] Luxembourg's focus on competencies and reputation of the management team rather than on the technical capabilities of the organization is a different tact than that usually taken in such laws and regulations. Of course, such issues may certainly be part of the authorization evaluation in numerous countries, but the lack of technical specification in the Luxembourg Law is exceptional.

Further, the requirement that two members of the management team have held formal high-level positions in the space industry or in a related sector could result in

9. Federal Communications Commission, "Mitigation of Orbital Debris in the New Space Age," 85 Fed. Reg. 52422-52454 (August 25, 2020).

newer start-ups seeking authorizations in jurisdictions with less stringent standards. These companies are often led by innovators with tight budgets, and the prospect of needing to hire senior executives for the sake of gaining authorization may be a burden that they would prefer to avoid. No comparable clauses can be found in similar space legislations of other countries.

While this clause is intended to limit the liability exposure of Luxembourg, its focus on reputational aspects of management rather than technical competencies of an organization seemingly fails to address liability exposure that could result from poor technical capabilities. While certainly, a management team that is mismanaging a company for its personal gain can place the State in a position of exposure, but so too could an operator run by a team with good repute but without the technical skills to properly operate in space.

Article 10 Risk Assessment and Insurance*

(1) The application for the authorization must be accompanied by a risk assessment of the mission. It shall specify the coverage of these risks by personal financial means, by an insurance policy of an insurance undertaking not belonging to the same group than the operator to be authorized or by a guarantee of a credit institution not belonging to the same group than the operator to be authorized.
(2) The authorization shall be conditional upon the existence of financial bases that are appropriate to the risks associated with the mission.

I. DRAFTING HISTORY

Article 10 of the 2017 Law on Space Resources focuses on the prevention of the risks inherent in any activity in space and is connected with the rules of responsibility for national space activities and liability for damage provided for in international space law, in particular in Articles VI and VII of the OST. In this relation, the financial stability of the applicant and future operator is a "critical issue,"[1] and consequently, the provision requires a financial soundness of the applicant.

The paragraph 2 of Article 10 was inspired by the notion of financial soundness set in Article 10 of the Draft, which was inspired by Article 8 of the 1993 Law on the Financial Sector[2] but without referring to specific numerical requirements. Article 10 links the justification of the financial assets of the applicant to their adequacy in relation to the risks relating to the mission, thereby leaving a wide margin of

* Laetitia Zarkan and P.J. Blount
1. 2016 Draft Law on Space Resources, p. 9.
2. 1993 Law on the Financial Sector, Art. 8(1):

> Authorization shall be conditional on the production of evidence showing the existence of an authorized capital of 8 700 000 EUR, of which 6 200 000 EUR must be fully paid up. Those amounts may be modified by Grand-Ducal regulation.

appreciation to the ministers responsible for issuing authorization.[3] The original text of the Article was accompanied by a provision giving the competence to specify the details of the required financial base of the operator to a Grand-Ducal regulation.

As for the form of the financial resources of the applicant, the text first stated that they must take not only the form of share capital but also, as a mandatory and cumulative obligation, the form of insurance or another guarantee that can be compared to insurance and that emanates either from an insurance company or a credit institution. The Draft added that the third party providing the guarantee must not belong to the same group as the applicant for the engagement agreement. A Grand-Ducal regulation was envisaged to specify the terms and conditions relating to the financial basis.[4]

In its opinion, the Chamber of Commerce considered that it would have been judicious to provide for a minimum amount, a percentage, or a range of required financial bases in the text of the Draft Law in order to allow private operators to evaluate their financial capacity in the field of the exploitation and use of space resources.[5]

The Conseil d'État reminded that the notion of "financial soundness of the applicant and of the shareholders and members referred to in paragraph 1" was inspired by Article 6(9)(c) of the 1993 Law on the Financial Sector without being strictly identical, since it refers to the financial soundness of the person who intends to acquire or increase the shareholding in a credit institution beyond certain thresholds. The Draft Law applies this notion to the applicant for authorization, a term that the Conseil d'État proposed to replace with "the operator to be licensed."[6] The Conseil d'État noticed that no amount is specified with regard to what can be considered as "financial soundness," leaving the ministers a flexibility to make the determination in this matter, but that it is simply required that the financial basis be able to "cover the risks related to the mission for which the authorization is sought." The Conseil d'État considered that such lack of precision of the amounts necessary to apply for a mission created legal uncertainty and formally objected to this provision.

Concerning the policy or guarantee be given by an insurance company or credit institution, the Conseil asked whether it can be limited to an insurance, or a credit institution established in a Member State of the European Union. The Conseil d'État demanded that the operator to be authorized should carry out a quantified evaluation of the direct and indirect risks of the exploration mission and of the use of the resources of outer space, specifying the coverage of these risks by the operator's own financial means and by the said insurance policy or guarantee. According to its opinion, such an evaluation should be supported by an independent expert evaluation if possible.[7] A serious criticism faced the provision of the original Draft vesting the competence to specify the details of the financial bases of the applicant to the Grand-Ducal regulation.

3. 2016 Draft Law on Space Resources, p. 9.
4. *Id.* at 14.
5. Avis de la Chambre de Commerce (January 10, 2017) 4.
6. Avis du Conseil d'État (April 7, 2017) 11.
7. *Id.* at 12.

Any issue connected with the freedom of commerce protected by the Constitution must be regulated by law and not by a sub-statutory regulation.[8]

The Commission of Economy debated the proposals of the Conseil d'État. For instance, the reference to the financial basis allows for more forms of coverage (share capital, insurance policy, comparable guarantee). The Commission considered that in this innovative and rapidly evolving sector, more flexibility would have been useful.[9] About the suggestion of the Conseil d'État to limit the policy or guarantee to those established in the European Union, the representatives of the Ministry disagreed with this recommendation. Referring to the experience acquired in the satellite sector, it would be counterproductive to limit this condition to credit and insurance entities established in a Member State of the European Union as they are "renowned actors" in this sector who are established elsewhere.[10]

In the new version of the Draft,[11] the Commission of Economy followed the suggestion of the Conseil d'État to require in the text that the operator to be authorized must carry out an upstream risk assessment and provide the details of the risk coverage and formulated accordingly the new paragraph 1 of the Article. As recommended by the Conseil d'État, the Commission also abolished the automatic accumulation of capital and insurance/guarantee, considering it would be better to let the future operator specify the risk coverage.[12]

However, the Commission argued that setting more or less arbitrarily a minimum or maximum amount of reference to establish the adequacy of the financial bases to the identified risks as required by the Conseil would not be relevant for space activities.[13] At the same time, it accepted the opinion of the Council and deleted the reference to the Grand-Ducal regulation intended to specify the details of these financial bases. Additionally, taking into account the specificity of this emerging sector, the new Draft did not implement the suggestion of the Conseil to limit itself to credit and insurance institutions established in a Member State of the European Union and instead, followed the argumentation of the representatives of the Ministry.

II. INTERPRETATION

In view of the risks inherent in any activity in space, the financial capacities of the applicant to respond to claims against it are an essential question. In view of these risks, the applicant is required by Article 10 to submit a risk assessment as part of its application for authorization. The 2017 Law on Space Resources gives no details as to how the risk assessment should be carried out, what factors should be taken into account in the risk assessment process, nor what risks should be evaluated.

8. *Id.* at 18.
9. Chambre des Députés, Commission de l'Economie, Procès-verbal de la réunion du 18 mai 2017, 4.
10. *Id.* at 5.
11. Amendements parlementaires (May 24, 2017).
12. Id. at 5.
13. *Id.*

Second, an applicant may demonstrate its ability to cover potential liability through three mechanisms. The company may self-insure if its capital and holdings are enough to cover the potential risk. It may also obtain either insurance to cover the risk or another guarantee that can be compared to insurance and that emanates from a credit institution. In the second two options, the third party providing the guarantee must not be affiliated with the applicant for engagement approval. The Law avoided limiting the choice of insurance institutions to the Member States of the European Union; therefore, the applicant can search for the guarantee globally.

Third, the applicant must evince financial bases that are appropriate to the risks associated with the mission. The Law does not give any instructions on this "appropriateness"; the Report of the Commission of Economy explains that the appropriateness would be measured on the basis of the information submitted by the applicant on a case-by-case basis, rather than arbitrarily setting up fixed limits which can appear inadequate in the course of time; this approach based on the scale of the risk is more modern and is more and more applied also in other sectors.[14]

III. EVALUATION

This clause provides the applicant some flexibility in how it chooses to cover the potential risks to third parties posed by its activities. This allows a company to scale their coverage based on the nature of their activities.

The idea of risk assessment is a critical part of authorization in a number of space laws globally, but there is no general harmonization about what should be required of a company. For instance, the US[15] and Japan[16] have both adopted systems of liability for launch service providers based on the calculation of a loss threshold for which the operator must gain insurance coupled with indemnity provided by the government beyond the insured value. Only a few States though require operators to insure against third-party risks across the life of a space operation as opposed to the launch phase, which is natural since the launch phase contains the highest risk for damage to the surface of the Earth. In the Belgian[17] and UK laws,[18] the authorizing authority "may" impose third-party liability insurance based on the risks posed by the mission. On the other hand, the Dutch law does require operators to obtain insurance to cover potential third-party damage as well as submit documentation on the solvency of the organization.[19]

The content of the provisions dealing with the risk assessment and the coverage of the risk in the 2020 Law on Space Activities is similar to the 2017 Law on Space Resources.

14. Chambre des Députés, Rapport de la Commission de l'Economie (July 6, 2017) 13.
15. 14 C.F.R. 440.
16. Hiroshi Kataoka, "Japanese Space Law—Legislation on Space Activities," presentation before 49th session COPUOS Legal Subcommittee (2010) https://www.unoosa.org/pdf/pres/lsc2010/tech-07.pdf.
17. 2005 Belgium Space Law, Art. 5(2).
18. UK Space Industry Act 2018, Art. 38.
19. 2006 Netherlands Space Activities Law, s. 3.

Article 11 Auditors*

(1) The authorization shall be conditional on the operator to be authorized having its annual accounts audited by one or more approved auditors who can show that they possess adequate professional experience.
(2) Any change in the auditors must be authorized in advance by the ministers.
(3) The rules in respect of commissaires, which may form a supervisory board as laid down in the Law of 10 August 1915 on commercial companies, as amended, only apply to operators where the Law on commercial companies mandatorily prescribes it even if there is an auditor.

I. DRAFTING HISTORY

Article 11 of the 2017 Law on Space Resources deals with external audit of annual accounts of the operator. It is based on the text of Article 10 of the 1993 Law on the Financial Sector.[1] Concerning the appointment of the auditors, the 1993 Law requires that these are appointed by the body responsible for managing the credit institution. The Conseil d'État suggested that the auditors be appointed by the assembly of shareholders of the operator and not by the administrative body as it is the case in the 1993 Law on the Financial Sector;[2] however, this suggestion cannot be found in the

* Laetitia Zarkan and P.J. Blount

1. 1993 Law on the Financial Sector, Art. 10:

    (1) Authorization shall be conditional on the institution having its annual accounts audited by one or more external auditors who can show that they possess adequate professional experience. Those external auditors shall be appointed by the body responsible for managing the credit institution.
    (2) Any change in the external auditors must be authorized in advance by the CSSF in accordance with Article 7(3).
    (3) Neither the rules in respect of auditors as laid down in the Law on commercial companies, nor Art. 137 of the Law of August 10, 1915, as amended, shall apply to credit institutions.

2. Avis du Conseil d'État (April 7, 2017) 13.

final text of the Article. On the recommendation of the Conseil d'État, a third paragraph has been added to the wording of Article 10 concerning the supervisory board of commercial companies.

II. INTERPRETATION

As a further condition for gaining an authorization of a space resource mission, a future operator must submit an external audit of its annual accounts. This is not a single audit that is submitted as a part of the application, but an ongoing requirement to ensure the liquidity of the organization throughout the life of the authorized mission.

The auditors must be able to demonstrate that they possess adequate professional experience. They have to be approved by the Ministry and cannot be changed without its approval.

According to Article 11(3), in cases in which the 1915 Law on Commercial Companies[3] envisages a company to have a supervisory board of commissaires, the operators to be authorized according to the 2017 Law on Space Resources have to comply with this condition only if the 1915 Law makes this condition compulsory.

III. EVALUATION

Article 10 provides an ongoing obligation to an authorized company to show that it is solvent. This makes sense with regard to the origins of the 2017 Law on Space Resources in the banking and financial legislation of Luxembourg. It also, though, serves to help protect the State against situations such as that of Iridium, which went bankrupt in 2002 with a constellation of satellites in orbit.[4] Concerns about the financial stability of the operators can be read also in the report on the negotiation of the Commission of Economy preceding the formulation of the final text of the Law. A representative of the Ministry of Economy stated that the Ministry is aware of the possibility of commercial failures of the operators. This is the reason why the authorization process must regulate the availability of financial bases covering the space resources missions during their whole duration.[5]

As can be confirmed by the plural "annual accounts," it is notable that presenting external audit is an ongoing obligation. A number of space laws, such as the 2006 Netherlands Space Activities Law,[6] require applicants to submit financial information about their organization; but an ongoing, annual auditing requirement may be unique

3. Law of August 10, 1915 on Commercial Companies, as consolidated by the Regulation of December 5, 2017.
4. *See generally* John Bloom, *Egocentric Orbits: The Iridium Story* (Grove Press: New York, 2016).
5. Chambre des Députés, Commission de l'Economie, Procès-verbal de la réunion du 11 mai 2017, 3.
6. 2006 Netherlands Space Activities Law, s. 3.

to Luxembourg. Presumably, such an auditing requirement will assist authorities in making an ongoing determination as to whether the operator remains financially sound enough to operate its on-orbit assets without risk to Luxembourg.

Article 12 Further Specifications*

The authorization shall describe the manner in which the operator to be authorized fulfils the conditions of articles 6 to 11, paragraph 1. It may in addition include provisions on:

a) the activities to be carried on within the territory of the Grand Duchy or from such territory;
b) the limits that could be associated with the mission;
c) the modalities for the supervision of the mission;
d) the conditions for ensuring compliance by the operator to be authorized with its obligations.

I. DRAFTING HISTORY

Article 12 established the requirement for specifications to be attached to any approval, following the example of Article 20 of the 1991 Electronic Media Law.[1] In line with this Law, the 2016 Draft Law on Space Resources provided for a "book of obligations,"[2] which was envisaged to specify how the applicant should meet the conditions required for obtaining the authorization. The text first added, in a nonexhaustive list, that the specifications may contain provisions on the fees to be paid, on the activities to be carried out in or from Luxembourg, on the limits of the mission or on the conditions aimed at ensuring that the operator complies with its obligations. The Commentary to the Draft explained that "the book of obligations may for example contain provisions on the long-term sustainability of space activities or the prevention of contamination of celestial bodies or adverse changes to the earth's environment"[3] when issuing specifications related to the approval. The aim of the Draft was to provide the ministers in

* Laetitia Zarkan and P.J. Blount
1. Mémorial A N° 42 (July 30, 1991).
2. In French: *Cahier des charges*.
3. 2016 Draft Law on Space Resources, 10.

charge with an instrument that allows them to clearly define the specific framework for each mission and the terms and conditions of monitoring.[4]

In its 2017 Opinion,[5] the Conseil d'État reminded that by taking over the some of the conditions required by the 1991 Electronic Media Law, the 2016 Draft Law on Space Resources did not set up an authorization or approval procedure for a future operator of a Luxembourg satellite system, but rather established a concession mechanism, implying that the licensor exercises rights over what it grants. It is in this context, the Conseil d'État stated that setting a concession system for outer space resources would be in contradiction with Article II of the OST, which prohibits any national appropriation of outer space and therefore formally opposed the Article, considering that it did not respect the primacy of international law.[6]

Thereafter, in order to meet the formal opposition expressed by the Conseil d'État, the Commission of Economy abandoned the concept of the "book of obligations" and formulated the additional conditions that may accompany the authorization directly in the text of the Article. It also decided to deal with the question of the fee to be charged in a separate article.[7]

II. INTERPRETATION

Article 12 prescribes that the authorization specifies the manner (*la manière*) in which the applicant—the operator to be authorized—fulfills the conditions of the authorization. This is an obligation imposed to the authorizing minister and can be understood as a duty to enumerate in a transparent manner the grounds leading to the decision, in accordance with the Luxembourg administrative procedure.[8] The authorization "may" require information in addition to that provided on the basis of Articles 6-11. To this end, the text then provides a nonexhaustive list of provisions that can be additionally included by the authorizing authority.

First, according to Article 12(a), the authorization may include an articulation of the activities to be carried out in or from the territory of Luxembourg. This provision is inspired by Article 20(7) of the 1991 Electronic Media Law and can be interpreted through analogy with the practice on the basis of this Article.

Second, the authorization may include provisions on the "limits" to be associated with the mission. It would be interesting to see whether these constrains correspond to the "technical constrains" as formulated by the 1991 Electronic Media Law in relation to the configuration of satellite system or whether other environmental constrains are meant.

Third, the authorization may formulate provision on the modalities for the supervision of the mission. If the model of this paragraph would be the 1991 Law on

4. *Id.* at 10.
5. Opinion of the Conseil d'État (April 7, 2017) 13.
6. *Id.* at 19.
7. Amendements parlementaires (May 24, 2017) 6.
8. Loi réglant la procédure administrative non contentieuse, Mémorial A N° 87 (December 27, 1978); Règlement grand-ducal relatif à la procédure à suivre par les administrations relevant de l'État et des communes, Mémorial A N° 54, July 6, 1979.

Electronic Media, the activity of the operator would be monitored by one more government commissioners (Article 20 of the 1991 Law). However, the 2017 Law on Space Resources entails a specific provision on supervision of the authorized missions in Article 15 that is decisive for this procedure. Consequently, this provision will be commented in the part dealing with Article 15.

Fourth, the authorization may encompass conditions for ensuring compliance by the operator to be authorized with its obligations. These duties may include the compliance of the operator with international obligations of Luxembourg as required by Article 2(3) of the 2017 Law on Space Resources. Furthermore, an authorization could contain provisions limiting the environmental impacts of the activity whether they be terrestrial or in space. This provision might have been inspired by Article 11 of the 2002 Law amending the Law on the Financial Sector[9] which regulated electronic money institutions.

III. EVALUATION

Article 12 adopts a flexible notion of what must be included in a granted authorization. In the first instance it must include information that is required in the statute, but it can also be at the discretion of the authorizing minister place other limitations or requirements on a particular mission. This is a particularly important power given to the minister or ministers as it allows adaptability based on the nature or type of mission being authorized. This discretion allows the Ministry latitude in making determinations across a range of space activities, since a one-size-fits-all approach to authorization creates rigidity that can limit the industry or put the State at risk of responsibility or liability. As new space applications proliferate, this adaptability will be crucial for enabling innovative technologies.

It could be argued that this clause introduces uncertainty in the authorization process and that an applicant will be unsure of what types of additional provision may be attached to its authorization. However, such provisions will likely be the result of bilateral discussions between the applicant and the Ministry, and more likely could lead to authorization of activities that would be denied without this flexibility.

9. Law of May 14, 2002 transposing into the Law of April 5, 1993 on the Financial Sector, as amended: Directive 2000/28/EC amending Directive 2000/12/EC relating to the taking up and pursuit of the business of credit institutions; Directive 2000/46/EC on the taking up, pursuit of and prudential supervision of the business of electronic money institutions, Mémorial A 2002, N° 51, Art. 11:

> Electronic money institutions, which started to carry on their business in Luxembourg before the date of entry into force of this Law or before 27 April 2002, if that date occurs in the interim, shall be deemed to be authorized. Such institutions shall be required to provide the CSSF with all such information as the CSSF may consider relevant in order for it to establish, within six months from the date of entry into force of this Law, whether they satisfy the requirements of this Law, to determine the measures to be taken so as to ensure compliance with those requirements, or to decide whether the authorization should be withdrawn.

Article 13 Fee*

For each application for an authorization, a fee shall be set by the ministers in order to cover the administrative expenses incurred in relation to the processing of the application. Such fee shall range from 5.000 to 500.000 euros depending on the complexity of the application and the amount of work involved.

A Grand-Ducal regulation shall determine the procedure applicable to the collection of such fee.

I. DRAFTING HISTORY

In the original Draft Law on Space Resources, the provision on the fee covering administrative expenses was included in the provision regulating additional conditions included in the authorization. The requirement on a fee was formulated in a flexible manner: The envisaged book of obligation "might" have contained a provision on the fee to the Public Treasury to be paid "when appropriate."

The question of the fee was subject of detailed evaluations of the Conseil d'État.[1] First, it stated that it is wrong to require the fee in a flexible manner (when appropriate). Second, it stated that in light of the criteria identified in its Opinion of November 18, 2014 on the Draft Law on the Implementation of the Package for Future—part one, the "fee" is in fact a quota tax, "defined as a mandatory levy for the provision of a public service,"[2] explaining that the payment of such a fee would be compulsory in return for a service that is sometimes imposed and sometimes simply made available.[3]

Recalling its Opinion of November 18, 2014, the Conseil d'État stated, "The Constitutional Court held in a judgment of March 2, 2007 (No 38/07) 'that in tax

* Laetitia Zarkan and P.J. Blount

1. Avis du Conseil d'État (April 7, 2017) 19.
2. Opinion of the Conseil d'État, November 18, 2014 on the Draft Law on the Implementation of the Package for Future, Part 1, p. 12, https://conseil-etat.public.lu/content/dam/conseil_etat/fr/avis/2014/11/50_833/50833.pdf.
3. *Id.* at 14.

matters the law must lay down the essential rules concerning the basis, rate and collection of the tax.'"[4] According to the Conseil d'État,[5] if the authors of the Draft decided to maintain the requirement of payment by the operator of a "fee" which is in fact a quota tax, the amount of this fee, or at least a minimum and a maximum amount, should be included in the text of the Law, on pain of formal opposition on the basis of Article 102 of the Constitution.[6]

Based on the Opinion of the Conseil, the Commission of Economy formulated a new article to deal with the fee.[7]

II. INTERPRETATION

Article 12 as adopted by the Parliament requires from the future operator of a space resources mission a payment of a fee "for each application for an authorization." There is no exemption from this obligation. The purpose of the fee is to cover "the administrative expenses" incurred in relation to the processing of the application. The obligation and the amount of the fee will be set by the authorizing ministers; the details of the procedure of collection of the fee will be determined by the Grand-Ducal regulation. For the application fee, the statute adopts a range between EUR 5,000 and EUR 500,000. The criteria for determining the payment are the complexity of the application and the amount of the work spent by the Ministry.

III. EVALUATION

The most noticeable feature of this Article is the extent of the range of fees that could be requested by the authorizing Ministry. The low end of EUR 5,000 is likely reasonable for most enterprises, where the high end of EUR 500,000 could be a significant burden to all but the most established corporations.

The fee paid is dependent on the complexity of the application and the work involved in the application. This is interesting in light of the information required from an applicant by the statute, most of which is standard business operations information. Article 6 of the Law does require a "mission plan" to be submitted, which is the likely place for complexity to be introduced. Presumably this requires the applicant to provide detailed information about the mission itself rather than the entity seeking authorization. There is then a question as to whether this provision may incentivize applicants to be less forthcoming in order to reduce the complexity of their application as a way to reduce the potential authorization fee.

4. Judgment of the Constitutional Court, March 2, 2007 (No. 38/07).
5. Avis du Conseil d'État (April 7, 2017) 14.
6. Constitution of Luxembourg, Art. 102.
7. Amendements parlementaires (May 24, 2017) 6 and Chambre des Députés, Rapport de la Commission de l'Economie (July 6, 2017) 83.

Another question, which will likely be addressed in the regulation, is at what point the fee is assessed. Presumably, the authorizing Ministry can only know the complexity of the application and the needed work after processing the application. If fees are assessed in this manner, then applicants may seek authorization in other States with more predictable fee structures.

Article 14 Withdrawal of Authorization*

(1) The authorization shall be withdrawn if the conditions for the granting thereof are no longer met.
(2) The authorization shall be withdrawn if the operator does not make use thereof within thirty-six months of it being granted, renounces to it or has ceased to carry out his business for the preceding six months.
(3) The authorization shall furthermore be withdrawn if it has been obtained through false statements or through any other irregular means.

I. DRAFTING HISTORY

Article 14 of the 2017 Law on Space Resources has not been the subject of substantial amendments during the legislative process leading to the adoption of the Law, other than the harmonization of the terminology used throughout the text. The provision is based on the conditions of withdrawal of authorization determined in the 1993 Law on the Financial Sector, as amended.[1]

During the reviewing process, the Conseil d'État considered the explanations accompanying the Draft Article and noted that the intention behind paragraph 1 was to *inter alia* ensure the operator's compliance with Luxembourg's international obligations.[2] In the Conseil d'État's Opinion, provision needed to be made more explicit regarding the operator's obligation to comply with international law.[3] The parliamentary Commission of Economy, which was in charge of reworking the text following the legislative reviewing process, agreed with the Conseil d'État and followed its advice to amend Article 2 paragraph 3 of the Draft Law to include the obligation to carry out the activity in accordance with *inter alia* "the international obligations of Luxembourg."[4]

* Gabrielle Leterre
1. 2016 Draft Law on Space Resources, Art. 13 and 1993 Law on the Financial Sector, Art. 11.
2. Avis du Conseil d'État (April 7, 2017) 14.
3. *Id.*
4. Chambre des Députés, Rapport de la Commission de l'Economie (July 6, 2017) 10.

The Conseil d'État further remarked that the expression "does not make use [of the authorization]" in paragraph 2 was unclear. In particular, it questioned whether "making use of" the authorization meant that the activity had to have started within the time allocated or if still being in the planning stages of the mission was sufficient to fulfill the criterion.[5] However, the Commission of Economy noted that the expression was taken from the 1993 Law on the Financial Sector and made no amendments.[6] The Conseil d'État made no further observation on this matter in its second Opinion.[7]

II. INTERPRETATION

Article 14 of the 2017 Law on Space Resources sets the conditions under which the mission authorization for the exploration and utilization of space resources can be withdrawn. First, pursuant to paragraph 1, the authorization shall be withdrawn if the conditions that led to the authorization being delivered are "no longer met." Remarkably, the provision does not pertain to what is commonly called a "fundamental change of circumstances" according to the explanations accompanying the Draft Article.[8]

A "change of circumstances" commonly refers to cases when circumstances that were ground for an agreement to be concluded between two, or more, parties have drastically changed and were not foreseen. This change of circumstances can then justify a party withdrawing from the agreement if the original circumstances—on which the agreement was based—were essential to the parties' consent to be legally bound or if their outcome radically changes the obligations agreed upon.[9] Interestingly, withdrawal based on a change of circumstances was considered in formulation of the general Law on Space Activities (Article 9) and, ultimately, removed from the Draft.[10] In particular, the text contemplated the withdrawal of the mission authorization when the new circumstances could bring about increased risks regarding the "safety of people and goods, the preservation of the environment, the international responsibility of the State or the strategic, economic and financial interests of the Luxembourgish State or the respect of its international obligations."[11]

In the present case, however, Article 14, paragraph 1 refers to a withdrawal of the authorization grounded in a violation by the operator of its legal obligations. Here, the Law aims at the compliance of the operator with its obligations under the mission authorization, the 2017 Law on Space Resources, Luxembourgish law and international law, such as the United Nations Space Treaties ratified by Luxembourg.[12]

5. Avis du Conseil d'État (April 7, 2017) 14.
6. Chambre des Députés, Rapport de la Commission de l'Economie (July 6, 2017) 10.
7. Avis complémentaire du Conseil d'État (June 27, 2017).
8. 2016 Draft Law on Space Resources, Art. 13, p. 10.
9. *See, e.g.*, Vienna Convention on the Law of Treaties, entered into force January 27, 1980, Art. 62, 1155 U.N.T.S. 331.
10. 2018 Draft Law on Space Activities, Art. 9, para. 2.
11. 2020 Draft Law on Space Activities, Art. 9, para. 1.
12. *Id.* As of January 2021, Luxembourg is a Signing Party to three of the five UN Space Treaties: the Treaty on Principles Governing the Activities of States in the Exploration and Use of Outer Space, Including the Moon and Other Celestial Bodies, entered into force on October 10, 1967, 610 U.N.T.S. 205 (Outer Space Treaty); the Convention on International Liability for Damage Caused

Accordingly, operators must *inter alia* refrain from appropriating celestial bodies in part or as a whole, show due regard to other operators' activities in outer space and avoid causing harmful contamination of the outer space environment.[13]

Paragraph 2 of Article 14 of the 2017 Law on Space Resources considers three more legal grounds for withdrawal: first, when the operator willingly renounces to the mission authorization; second, when the operator "has ceased to carry out its business" for the last six months, for instance due to the dissolution of the commercial entity; third, when the operator has not "made use" of the authorization during the first three years following the time of obtaining the authorization.

The last instance might be the most obscure of the three, as stressed by the Conseil d'État.[14] There is no indication of what "making use" of the mission authorization entails exactly. In the context of the 2017 Law on Space Resources, is it to be interpreted as operators having started extracting resources? Or as them having launched an object in space to map out what resources are in place? Does planning the mission or hiring personnel make use of the authorization?[15] There is no definitive answer.

However, paragraph 2 mirrors Article 11 of the 1993 Law on the Financial Sector, which also allows for withdrawal when the authorization is not used.[16] In practice, the goal of the provision is to avoid having an authorization that lays "dormant."[17] Thus, it is unlikely that operators will see their authorization withdrawn if the mission is still in the planning stage, so long as the intent to carry out the mission can be proven.

Lastly, paragraph 3 allows for the withdrawal of the mission authorization when operators obtained it "through false statements or through any other irregular means." This last paragraph considers cases where the consent to grant the authorization was corrupted. In particular, "false statements" refer to *inter alia* the information that must accompany the request for a mission authorization such as: the central administration of the commercial entity being situated in Luxembourg, the identity of the shareholders who must be knowledgeable and of good repute, and the risk assessment report.[18]

III. EVALUATION

Article 14 of the 2017 Law on Space Resources is in line with similar provisions relating to the withdrawal of authorization in of other national legislations regulating space

by Space Objects, entered into force on October 9, 1973, 961 U.N.T.S. 187 (Liability Convention); and the Convention on Registration of Objects Launched into Outer Space, entered into force on September 15, 1976, 1023 U.N.T.S. 15 (Registration Convention). Luxembourg is also working on becoming a Party to the Agreement on the Rescue of Astronauts, the Return of Astronauts, and the Return of Objects Launched into Outer Space, entered into force on December 3, 1968, 672 U.N.T.S. 119 (Return and Rescue Agreement).

13. *See* Outer Space Treaty, Arts. II and IX.
14. Avis du Conseil d'État (April 7, 2017) 14.
15. *Id.*
16. 1993 Law on the Financial Sector, Art. 11.
17. Elisabeth Omes, "PSA—PSF: Convergences et Divergences," in *Les Professionnels du Secteur des Assurances au Luxembourg. Les Apports de la Loi du 12 juillet 2013* (Kluwer 2014) 117, 125-126.
18. 2017 Law on Space Resources, Arts. 7-12.

activities. However, several foreign legislations also provide for the withdrawal of the authorization in cases when it contravenes to national interests.[19]

Furthermore, it is worth to note that other national legislations further allow for the (temporary) suspension of the mission authorization, such as in South Africa,[20] the United Kingdom[21] and France.[22]

19. 1993 South African Space Act; 2021 UK Space Industry Regulations, Art. 15; 2008 French Space Act, Art. 9; and 2005 Belgian Space Law, Art. 11.
20. 1993 South African Space Act, Art. 13.
21. 2021 UK Space Industry Regulations, Art. 15.
22. 2008 French Space Act, Art. 9.

Article 15 Supervision*

The ministers are in charge of the continuous supervision of the missions for which an authorization has been granted.

I. DRAFTING HISTORY

Article 15 of the 2017 Law on Space Resources establishes the internal legal basis for the continuous supervision of authorized space resource activities in Luxembourg. Within the original Draft Law,[1] this provision was laid down in Article 14, which was also significantly longer. On June 15, 2017, the Commission of Economy shortened the text[2] to implement the recommendations made by the Conseil d'État in its Opinion of April 7, 2017.[3] On July 31, 2017, the Article was renumbered to 15 pursuant to the addition of a new Article 13 by the Chamber of Deputies.[4]

The original text of Article 15 (former Article 14) included an additional sentence in the first paragraph providing the possibility for the minister(s) to be assisted by one or more Governmental commissioners.[5] According to the Conseil, the legal basis for this power shall be found in the attributions granted to the ministers under the concession's system, which used to be the one chosen for space communication.[6] Therefore, the Conseil formally opposed its inclusion in this Law as incompatible with the authorization system chosen for the regulation of space resource activities.[7] To comply with the Conseil's decision, on June 15, 2017 the Commission of Economy removed this sentence from the Law.[8]

* Antonino Salmeri
1. 2016 Draft Law on Space Resources, p. 5.
2. Amendements parlementaires (May 24, 2017) 7.
3. Avis du Conseil d'État (April 7, 2017) 15.
4. Chambre des Députés, Rapport de la Commission de l'Economie (July 6, 2017) 10-11.
5. 2016 Draft Law on Space Resources, p. 5.
6. Avis du Conseil d'État (April 7, 2017) 15.
7. *Id.*
8. Amendements parlementaires (May 24, 2017) 7.

The original text of Article 15 (former Article 14) also included a second paragraph according to which the minister(s) had the power to "impose additional conditions in accordance with the provisions of this law to a mission which they have previously authorized."[9] The Conseil found this provision highly confusing as to the exact nature and substance of these additional conditions.[10] Given the lack of proper clarity and justifications, the Conseil deemed this paragraph to be in conflict with Article 11(6) of the Constitution of Luxembourg as a restriction to the freedom of commerce, and thus formally opposed its inclusion.[11] To comply with the Conseil's Opinion, on June 15, 2017, the Commission of Economy removed this paragraph from the Law.[12]

II. INTERPRETATION

Article 15 establishes that the minister(s) authorizing a space resource mission are also in charge of its continuous supervision.[13] This provision complements Article 2 of the 2017 Law on Space Resources, according to which the exploration or use of space resources can only be conducted pursuant to a written authorization from the competent ministers.[14] In accordance with the above-described drafting history of the provision, this supervision shall be exercised directly by the competent Ministry based upon applicable legal requirements as well as the conditions explicitly stated in the authorization granted to the operator.

As discussed under Article 2 of the Commentary on the 2017 Law on Space Resources, both Articles implement the international obligations stemming from Article VI of the OST, according to which private activities in space shall require the authorization and continuing supervision of the appropriate State, which shall also assure their conformity to the OST provisions.[15] The State's duty to authorize and continuingly supervise private space activities is an essential safeguard for the respect of international law in outer space and celestial bodies.[16] It is important to note that the duty to supervise implies an obligation of due diligence,[17] which means that States have to actively verify the legitimate conduct of private activities in outer space.[18]

9. 2016 Draft Law on Space Resources, p. 5.
10. Avis du Conseil d'État (April 7, 2017) 15.
11. *Id.*
12. Amendements parlementaires (May 24, 2017).
13. 2017 Law on Space Resources, Art. 15.
14. *Id.* at Art. 2.
15. Outer Space Treaty, Art. VI.
16. Tanja Masson-Zwaan, "Article VI of the Outer Space Treaty and Private Human Access to Space," in *Proceedings of the 51st Colloquium on the Law of Outer Space* (2009) 537.
17. Bin Cheng, *Studies in International Space Law* (2004) 150-211 and Antonio Cassese, *International Law* (2005) 168.
18. Masson-Zwaan, "Article VI," 537.

III. EVALUATION

Article 15 is in line with comparable provisions from other existing national space legislations on space resource activities. Section 402 of the 2015 US CSLCA promotes the right of US citizens to engage in space resource activities "in accordance with the international obligations of the United States and subject to authorization and continuing supervision by the Federal Government."[19] Similarly, Article 18 of the 2019 UAE FLRSS[20] entrusts the Council of Ministers with the power to determine "the conditions and controls" of permits for exploration and use of space resources. Interestingly, in all these cases the definition of the actual powers available for the supervision of space resource activities has been deferred to future implementing regulations.

19. 2015 US CSLCA, s. 402.
20. 2019 UAE FLRSS, Art. 18.

Article 16 Liability for Damage*

The operator that is granted an authorization for a mission is fully responsible for any damage caused at the occasion of the mission, including at the occasion of all preparatory works and duties.

I. DRAFTING HISTORY

Article 16 of the 2017 Law on Space Resources was adopted without amendments. In the opinion of the Conseil d'État, the provision was superfluous and could have been removed entirely from the Law because there is no reason to doubt that the operators are liable for any damage they may cause.[1] The Conseil d'État also observed that the majority of activities would most likely take place outside of Luxembourg's territory and that, as such, there was no certainty liability would be decided under Luxembourgish law.

It further noted that Article 16 did not exclude Luxembourg's international responsibility pursuant to Article VI of the OST and that the State is primarily responsible and liable for damages caused. It can, however, turn against the operator to bear the consequences of the liability.

The Commission of Economy agreed with the remarks of the Conseil d'État but considered that a reminder that operators are liable for the damage they cause was useful considering the specificity of economic activities in the emerging space sector.[2]

II. INTERPRETATION

Article 16 of the 2017 Law on Space Resources reaffirms the full and sole liability of operators when a damage occurs while carrying out the activity covered by the mission authorization. Accordingly, operators are held liable during all the phases of the

---

* Gabrielle Leterre
1. Avis du Conseil d'État (April 7, 2017) 8.
2. Chambre des Députés, Rapport de la Commission de l'Economie (July 6, 2017) 10-11.

activity, from the preparatory stages to the end of the mission, including dealing with the end of life of space objects used during the activity.

In this instance, Article 16 brings clarity to the financial risk operators must bear in the application of Articles VI and VII of the OST. As the State authorizing the mission and the launch of space objects in the framework of the authorized activity, Luxembourg is internationally responsible and liable for the actions of its operators. As such, when an operator violates one of Luxembourg's international obligations or causes damage while carrying out activities in space, Luxembourg officially assumes the responsibility for their activities.

However, in practice, it is common for the State to turn to the faulty operators and make them bear the financial consequences of the damage, albeit not always in the full scale as Luxembourg. By explicitly holding the operator liable in Article 16, Luxembourg does not clear itself of liability under international law; rather it integrates plainly, in its legal framework, a domestic common practice. This is further confirmed by reading Article 16 in conjunction with Article 10 paragraph 2 which relates to the obligation of operators to prove they can assume the financial risks of their activity in space. Article 10 of the 2017 Law on Space Resources makes the delivery of the mission authorization "conditional upon the existence of financial bases that are appropriate to the risks associated with the mission." It requires operators to conduct a risk assessment when applying for the authorization and to present proof that they are able to cover the identified risks "by personal financial means, by an insurance policy ... or by a guarantee of a credit institution ... ."[3]

Regrettably, the 2017 Law on Space Resources does not specify what type of damage is covered under the text. Nonetheless, since Luxembourg is a Party to the Liability Convention and taking into account the purpose of Article 16, it can be assumed that the term "damage" is understood in a similar manner as in the Convention. That is, it covers "loss of life, personal injury or other impairment of health; or loss of or damage to property of States or of persons, natural or juridical, or property of international intergovernmental organizations."[4]

III. EVALUATION

The comment from the Conseil d'État that Article 16 appeared superfluous because of its "obviousness"[5] is in line with what can be seen in foreign space legislations. When dealing with issues of liability, the great majority of national space legislations do not explicitly mention that the operator is liable. Rather, they focus their attention on operators having liability insurance or exhibiting the financial responsibility to compensate for the damage they caused while carrying out the activity defined in the mission authorization.[6]

3. 2017 Law on Space Resources, Art. 10, para. 1.
4. Liability Convention, Art. I, para. a.
5. Avis du Conseil d'État (April 7, 2017) 15.
6. For example, National and Commercial Space Programs, 51 U.S.C § 50914 (2012); Decree 5663-1 about Space Activity, No. 5663-1, Art. 25(1) (1993) (RU); 1993 South African Space Act, Art. 14.

Nevertheless, the reminder that the State may turn to the operators to bear the financial costs because they are held liable for the damage they cause under Article 16 is not entirely uncommon. Both France and Belgium take a step further in establishing the operator's liability by explicitly providing the State with a right for recourse against the operator in such circumstances.[7] However, contrary to the French and Belgian laws, the 2017 Law on Space Resources does not define the term "damage" in its text, which is particularly regrettable when considering it makes a point of recalling the liability of the operator. It is worth noting that the Luxembourg's 2020 general Law on Space Activities addresses this issue by defining, in Article 2, the term "damage," which covers "any harm to persons, property, public health or the environment directly caused by a space object within the scope of a space activity, excluding the consequences of use of the signal emitted by that object for users."

In contrast to numerous space legislations, the 2107 Law on Space Resources does not limit the amount of the licensee's liability.

7. 2005 Belgian Space Law, Art. 15; 2008 French Space Act.

Article 17 Other Authorizations*

The granting of an authorization for a mission does not dispense from the need to obtain other approvals or authorizations.

I. DRAFTING HISTORY

According to the Commentary to Article 17, "other approvals or authorizations" were to include primarily a business license.[1] In its 2017 Opinion, the Conseil d'État noted that the conditions of authorization were inspired by the 1993 Law on the Financial Sector, specifically by the conditions required for establishment of credit institutions.[2] However, once authorized, the credit institutions do not need to be in possession of a (additional) authorization pursuant to the 2011 Law regulating Access to the Professions of Craftsman, Trader, Industrialist and Certain Liberal Professions.[3] Therefore, the Conseil d'État considered that an authorization in application of the aforementioned Law of September 2, 2011 would not make sense in view of the conditions set out in the Draft Law, underlining that one may wonder under which category a company whose object is to exploit the "resources of space" could be classified.[4]

The Commission of Economy did not follow this position. The Ministry of Economy's representatives reaffirmed the importance of maintaining this Article, considering that the companies concerned may pursue also other activities than the missions covered by the proposed scheme, and would not only exploit the "resources of space." Therefore, as the authorization is limited to the specific mission, the

---

* Laetitia Zarkan and Mahulena Hofmann

1. 2016 Draft Law on Space Resources.
2. 1993 Law on the Financial Sector, pp. 462 ff.
3. Law of September 2, 2011 Regulating Access to the Professions of Craftsman, Trader, Industrialist and Certain Liberal Professions, Mémorial A N° 198 (September 2, 2011).
4. Avis du Conseil d'État (April 7, 2017) 8.

Commission of Economy decided to keep the Article, a decision that did not raise any further objections from the Conseil d'État.[5]

II. INTERPRETATION

This provision makes clear that an authorization under the Law on Space Resources does not mean that the applicant is free from obligations to get other authorizations that may be required by the legal order of Luxembourg. Which other authorizations will or will not be needed can be derived *per analogiam* from the *travaux préparatoires* to the 2020 Draft Law on Space Activities of Luxembourg containing identical provision in its Article 5(1).

The first Draft of the 2020 Law on Space Activities required that in addition to the authorization of a space resources mission, a specific authorization of the launching of space objects envisaged to be placed in outer space was necessary; however, this condition was deleted from the text because launching would be covered by the mission authorization. On the other hand, the discussions in the Commission of Economy showed a tendency to keep the provision on additional authorization meaning that a business license issued by the Ministry of the Middle Classes will be needed by each operator performing economic activities.[6]

The 2017 and 2020 space laws of Luxembourg did not abolish the 1991 Electronic Media Law. Therefore, another authorization or concession may be required in case the operator wishes to use a satellite system using frequencies allocated to Luxembourg. For using frequency spectrum, the operator may need an authorization (general or individual) issued by the Minister for Communication and Media[7] based on the 2021 Law on Electronic Communication.[8] In specific cases, an export control license may be required.

III. EVALUATION

As with any business enterprise, there is a complex of regulations that must be taken into account and public entities to be consulted in order to properly fit in the legal framework of a given country. In this line, Article 17 indicates that the authorization for space resources mission may not cover all aspects of the mission and does not

5. Chambre des Députés, Commission de l'Economie, Procès-verbal de la réunion du 18 mai 2017, p. 8.
6. P.V. ECOPC 14, p. 7.
7. According to the Decree of December 5, 2018, the Minister on Communications and Media remains responsible for the satellite systems of Luxembourg.
8. Loi du 17 décembre 2021 portant transposition de la directive (UE) 2018/1972 du Parlement européen et du Conseil du 11 décembre 2018 établissant le code des communication électroniques européen et portant modification de la loi modifiée du 30 mai 2005 portant 1) organisation de l'institut Luxembourgeois de Régulation; 2) modification de la loi modifiée du 22 juin 1963 fixant le régime des traitements des fonctionnaires de l'État, Mémorial A N° 927, December 22, 2021.

deprive the operator of the obligation to receive additional authorizations. For instance, in order to do business, a company will need a business license,[9] or in order to communicate with a spacecraft the company may need an authorization to use a particular frequency. The nature of the authorizations that an organization seeking authorization under this statute will need to obtain will, of course, depend a great deal on the nature and scope of the organization's business activities.

The fact that the provision gives no list of what other authorizations may be required may be a challenge for smaller companies not having their own legal specialist. In practice, this outcome can be overcome by creating a "one-shop" address where the information about all necessary authorization procedures would be concentrated.

9. Law of September 2, 2011 regulating Access to the Professions of Craftsman, Trader, Industrialist and Certain Liberal Professions, Mémorial A N° 198 (September 22, 2011), as amended.

Article 18 Sanctions*

(1) Any person who contravenes or attempts to contravene the provisions of article 2 shall be punished by a term of imprisonment of between eight days and five years and a fine of between 5.000 and 1.250.000 euros or either one of those penalties.
(2) Any person who contravenes or attempts to contravene the provisions of articles 5, 9 paragraph 3 subparagraph 1, 11 paragraph 1 or 2 or that contravenes the terms and conditions of the authorization shall be punished by a term of imprisonment of between eight days and one year and a fine of between 1.250 and 500.000 euros or either one of those penalties.
(3) Without prejudice to paragraphs 1 and 2, the court to which the matter is being referred, may declare the discontinuance of an operation contravening the provisions of the present law, under a penalty the maximum of which shall not exceed 1.000.000 euros per day of infringement found.

I. DRAFTING HISTORY

Article 18 of the 2017 Law on Space Resources has been the object of several substantial amendments at the recommendation of the Conseil d'État. It considered that the provision was not sufficiently thorough in listing obligations which violation could be criminally punished and that, consequently, it was not complying with the principle of legality under criminal law.[1] Thus, the Conseil d'État demanded, subject to formal opposition, amendments be made to paragraph 2 to refer more precisely to all such existing obligations in the text.

Similarly, the Draft provision did not have originally any written amount in paragraph 3. The maximum amount of the penalty was left to be decided by the jurisdiction ceased with the matter. However, the Conseil d'État noted that the

* Gabrielle Leterre
1. Avis du Conseil d'État (April 7, 2017) 16.

principle of the legality of sanctions under criminal law requires paragraph 2[2] to indicate the precise amount or a range of amount for the daily penalty of the infringement found.

Furthermore, the Conseil d'État suggested that the original paragraph 3 be removed. It read: "This article shall apply without prejudice to the penalties laid down by the Penal Code or by other individual laws."[3] The Commission of Economy agreed with the suggested amendments and proceeded accordingly.

II. INTERPRETATION

Article 18 of the 2017 Law on Space Resources makes a distinction between two types of offenses. Paragraph 1 defines sanctions for the violation of Article 2 of the Law, which sets the obligation to obtain from the minister in charge a written mission authorization to professionally explore and utilize space resources. This authorization is personal and does not allow for someone other than the designated operator to carry out the mission, not even an intermediary. Article 2 further recalls the obligation of the operator to comply with the conditions of the authorization and Luxembourg's international obligations, such as the one defines in the ratified UN Space Treaties. Anyone contravening these obligations, or attempting to, risks a term of imprisonment of between eight days and five years and/or a fine of between EUR 5,000 and EUR 1,250,000.

The second paragraph of Article 18 aims to punish anyone who leads or participates in a resource exploitation mission which violates the operator's other obligations under the present law. Also included in the scope of paragraph 2 are the compliance with the conditions and terms of the mission authorization; the maintaining of the operator's management body's good repute at all times, and the annual audit of the account by one or more adequate approved auditors (*réviseurs d'entreprises agréés*). Furthermore, any change of the auditor must, first, be authorized by the minister in charge. Any contravention, or attempt to contravene, these obligations expose the person to a term of imprisonment of between eight days and one year and/or a fine of between EUR 1,250 and EUR 500,000.

Additionally, pursuant to the third paragraph, the jurisdiction to which the matter is being referred may decide that the activity which is violating the Law must be ceased or be subjected to a penalty of maximum EUR 1,000,000 per each day of infringement.

III. EVALUATION

It is not uncommon for national space legislations to provide for civil and criminal sanctions for the violation of their terms. However, how these sanctions are defined in national laws varies. In some cases, the law refers back to the existing common regime

2. 2016 Draft Law on Space Resources, Art. 17, para. 4.
3. *Id.* at para. 3.

for civil and criminal offenses, with the addition of cap limits.[4] For instance, under the 2018 UK Space Industry Act the amount of the fine varies depending on if the summary conviction takes place in England and Wales or in Scotland or Northern Ireland.[5] In other cases, the State chose to define specific sanctions for violations linked to space activities. For instance, like Luxembourg, South Africa mixes the terms of imprisonment and fines depending on the nature of the obligation violated.[6] Article 18 of the 2017 Law on Space Resources also shares similitudes with Article 19 of the 2005 Belgian Space Act. Both provide term of imprisonment comprised between eight days and a year with the additional possibility of a fine.[7]

4. For example, Act on Space Activities, No. (63/2018), Art. 21 (2018) (FI); 2018 UK Space Industry Act, Arts. 51-59; Space Activities Act 1998 No. 123, Arts. 80-83 (1998) (AU).
5. 2018 UK Space Industry Act, Art. 53.
6. 1993 South African Space Act, Art. 23. *See also* 2008 French Space Act, Art. 11.
7. 2005 Belgian Space Law, Art. 1.

Chapter 2 Commentary on the 2020 Law on Space Activities

Article 1 Scope*

Article 1 is composed of two parts: Its first part contains the positive delimitation of the scope of the Law, whereas the second part expressly takes out space resources missions out of it. The two parts are commented consecutively.

Part 1:

This Law shall apply to space activities carried out:

1. **by an operator, whatever the nationality thereof, from the territory of the Grand Duchy of Luxembourg or by means or installations, whether movable or immovable, under the control and jurisdiction of the Grand Duchy of Luxembourg; or**
2. **in the territory of a foreign State or an area not subject to the sovereignty of a State by natural persons of Luxembourg nationality or by legal persons established under Luxembourg law.**

I. DRAFTING HISTORY

Before entering into force of the 2017 Law on Space Resources and the 2020 Law on Space Activities, space activities of Luxembourg were authorized according to the 1991 Electronic Media Law. This Law encompasses a regime of authorization of satellite systems that is based on governmental concession that allows the use of certain frequency bands and orbital positions (Article 20). The concession is accompanied by a book of obligations, and its implementation is monitored by one or more government commissioners. The scope of the 1991 Electronic Media Law is limited to "Luxembourgish satellite systems." These are systems of one or more satellites using the satellite

* Mahulena Hofmann

frequencies the Grand Duchy of Luxembourg that are entitled to exploit these frequencies in accordance with relevant international agreements (ITU), regardless of whether these frequencies belong to broadcasting or other service.[1]

This situation was principally satisfactory so long as SES, one of the largest global satellite operators, limited its principal activities to the transmission of radio and television programs using the frequencies allocated to Luxembourg. With the broadening of the scope of its interests to the transmission of data, broadband and navigation, and the expansion of space activities of Luxembourg into the New Space area, such as remote sensing or on-orbit servicing, the scope of Article 20 of the 1991 Electronic Media Law became inadequate for authorization. If an operator established in Luxembourg would have intended to use other than Luxembourgish frequencies, it could theoretically have launched a space object without any authorization from the Government of Luxembourg.[2] The Government was not only lacking any sufficient legal basis for authorizing the new forms of space activities but also a clear legal basis for refusing to authorize a space activity. This was worrying as it was obvious that the lack of a general authorization regime, including potentially risky space activities, neither deprived Luxembourg of its international responsibility for "national activities," nor of the potential liability for damage caused by space objects launched under its jurisdiction into outer space.

This situation called for the drafting a general Space Law to provide the Government with a broader regime of authorization covering all situations for which Luxembourg could become responsible and liable according to the relevant international treaties and also providing operators with a transparent and predicable regime to consider when planning their activities. Considering these aims, the original version of Article 1 submitted by the Minister for Communications and Media in June 2018[3] was formulated as follows: "The Law shall regulate space activities for which Luxembourg could be held responsible and liable according to the OST and the Liability Convention. It shall be applicable to space activities carried out from the Luxembourg territory or from movable or immovable installations under the jurisdiction or control of the Grand Duchy. Furthermore, it shall cover space activities carried out in other places by the Luxembourg's citizens or legal persons." This approach corresponded broadly to the UN Resolution 68/74, paragraph 2.[4]

This wide scope of the Draft was welcomed by the Chamber of Commerce, which underlined that it offers sufficient flexibility in covering new situations in the future.[5] The Conseil d'État, which also intervened substantially in the course of finalization of the 2017 Law on Space Resources,[6] took an opposite opinion. It expressly denied "any normative value" to the phrase connecting the future authorization regime with the potential international responsibility and liability of Luxembourg,[7] stressing that only

1. 1991 Electronic Media Law, Art. 2(27).
2. 2018 Draft Law on Space Activities, Exposé des motifs, p. 3.
3. *Id.*, at Art. 1.
4. 2018 Draft Law on Space Activities, Commentaire des articles.
5. Avis de la Chambre de commerce (November 19, 2018).
6. Avis du Conseil d'État (April 7, 2017).
7. Avis du Conseil d'État (February 15, 2019) 2-3: "n'a pas de valeur normative en tant que telle."

the two subsequent provisions were legally relevant. Concerning these provisions, it recommended that in case of space activities performed from the Luxembourg territory, a supplement "whatever (the) nationality (of the operator) may be" is added. Regarding the activities carried out from "other places" than Luxembourg's territory or places under its jurisdiction, the Conseil proposed that "other places" are replaced by "in the territory of a foreign State or an area not subject to the sovereignty of a State." In fact, these are "other places" (the UN Resolution uses the term "elsewhere"), but the Conseil preferred to follow strictly the 2008 French Space Act which operates with these terms.[8]

The parliamentary Commission for Economy, Protection of Consumers and Space shared the view of the Conseil in denying any normative value to the provision intended to cover expressly all cases of potential responsibility and liability of Luxembourg for its space activities.[9] However, in the discussion dealing with the question of deleting this provision from the proposal, the approach defining the scope of the Law through the extent of potential international responsibility and liability of Luxembourg reappeared through a back door. It was reminded that international responsibility of Luxembourg can be evoked not only by launching space objects from ships and maritime platforms but also from airplanes under the Luxembourg jurisdiction. Additionally, it was suggested that the term "legal persons established under Luxembourg law" should be read as "legal persons having their seat in Luxembourg."

The consolidated text of the proposal prepared by the Commission of Economy in September 2020 incorporated the recommendations of the Conseil d'État.[10] It deleted the provision describing the scope of the future law by the potential responsibility and liability of Luxembourg and accepted its proposal to use the formulations of the French Space Act. The final version of the project presented by the same Commission to the Parliament in December 2020 incorporated these modifications.[11] In its Commentary to the Articles, the Commission stressed at least two times that the present definitions "cover all situations for which Luxembourg may be responsible or liable in the future."

II. INTERPRETATION

The first two paragraphs of the 2020 Law on Space Activities require that following persons apply for an authorization issued by the Minister of Economy. First, they are operators of whatever nationality, planning to carry out a space activity from the Luxembourg territory or from installations under its control and jurisdiction. The question remains, whether also the activities of stateless persons are subject of the authorization procedure in Luxembourg. The original version, which avoided the term "nationality," was more flexible in this respect. What is Luxemburg territory is clear;

8. 2018 French Space Act.
9. Chambre des Députés, Commission de l'Economie, de la Protection des consommateurs et de l'Espace Procès-verbal de la réunion du 14 mai 2020.
10. Amendements parlementaires (July 20, 2020).
11. Rapport de la Commission de l'Economie, de la Protection des Consommateurs et de l'Espace (December 2, 2020).

the "installations under Luxembourg jurisdiction" are described by the Commentary to the Articles[12] as movable and immovable structures including all potential launching facilities. Explicitly mentioned in the Commentary to the Articles are airplanes under Luxembourg jurisdiction and control, ships in high seas, maritime, and space platforms. Interestingly, the motives do not mention launching of satellites from other space objects.

The second group of operators subjected to the authorization regime according to the Luxembourg space law are natural persons of Luxembourg nationality[13] and legal persons established under Luxembourg law[14] that are planning to carry out a space activity in the territory of a State other than Luxembourg. The provision remains open whether this activity also extends to the installations outside the territory of a foreign State but under its control and jurisdiction—such as airplanes, ships, maritime, and space platforms. In an analogy to paragraph 1, the simplest answer would be yes. Furthermore, an authorization is expressly needed also for space activities of Luxembourg nationals carried out in areas that are not subject to the sovereignty of a State, e.g., from the high seas. The question is whether this addition was urgently necessary. It seems that with the present state of technology, an activity will be always carried out from an installation attributable to a specific jurisdiction.[15]

Which activity must be authorized is determined by the definition of "space activities." According to Article 2 of the Law, these are the activities consisting in launching or attempting to launch objects in outer space, the control and use of space objects, return to the Earth, and any other activity for which Luxembourg is likely to be internationally liable. As no specific rule has been added concerning the obligation to complete an orbit, also the suborbital flights reaching outer space seem to be included in the definition.

III. EVALUATION

The positive determination of the scope of the general 2020 Law on Space Activities is a result of long deliberations and discussions. The transfer of the rule connecting this scope with international law, and specifically responsibility and liability of Luxembourg, to the definition of space activities is a legislative decision that is difficult to contest.

The replacement of the original rules setting aside the "nationality" of the operator, not specifying the "other places," and avoiding the "areas not subject to the sovereignty" by the provisions of the practice-proven 2008 French Space Act[16] was a practical solution. The first question is whether the original text was not more precise,

12. 2018 Draft Law on Space Activities, p. 7.
13. Law of March 8, 2017 on Luxembourg Nationality (Loi du 8 mars 2017 sur la nationalité luxembourgeoise), Mémorial A N° 289, March 17, 2017.
14. Law of December 21, 2017 regarding Commercial Companies (and Legal Persons' nationality), Loi du 10 aout 1915 concernant les sociétés commerciales (et nationalité de personne légale), Mémorial A N° 90, 30 octobre 1915.
15. *See, e.g.*, Art. 91(1) UNCLOS.
16. 2018 French Space Act, Art. 2.

and the second question is why the user of the Luxembourg law has to search in the commentaries of the 2008 French Space Act when seeking the precise meaning of the wording of the Article. Moreover, the 2008 French Space Act differentiates between the operators intending to launch space objects from the French territory, French operators intending to do so from foreign territories, and additionally the persons who intend to procure launching of space objects.

There are examples of other solutions. The 2011 Austrian Federal Law on the Authorisation of Space Activities[17] requires authorization for space activities performed on Austrian territory, on board of vessels or airplanes registered in Austria, or by natural person with Austrian citizenship or legal person seated in Austria. The 2017 Belgian Law on launch activities[18] covers the launching, operation and guidance of space objects carried out in areas under the Belgian jurisdiction or control or using its installation, personal or real property. When "provided for under an international agreement," this Law may apply to activities carried out by persons of Belgian nationality, irrespective of the location. The 2018 Act on Space Activities of Finland[19] relates to space activities carried on within the territory of the State of Finland extending to the space activities outside the territory of Finland if performed on board a vessel or aircraft registered in Finland or by Finish citizens or legal persons incorporated in Finland. The recent 2019 Decree-Law of Portugal[20] applies to space activities in national territory, including the maritime area and the airspace, vessels, aircraft, and facilities under Portuguese jurisdiction, irrespective of nationality of the operator and to activities performed outside the national territory by Portuguese operators or operators established in the national territory.

This overview shows that the original definition of the Luxembourg law describing the scope of the document as all situations in which Luxembourg may be internationally responsible and liable, was not incorrect. The question whether it was "without any legal value" can be further debated: A reference to international law provisions in the domestic law is a relatively usual method of harmonization of national legal order with international law that is not exclusive to space law.

Part 2:

This Law shall not apply to missions involving the exploration and use of space resources governed by the Law of 20 July 2017 on the exploration and use of space resources, except for Articles 15 and 16, paragraph 2.

17. 2011 Austrian Federal Law on the Authorisation of Space Activities and the Establishment of a National Space Registry (Outer Space Act), adopted by the National Council on December 6, 2011, entered into force on December 28, 2011.
18. Belgium, 2017 Law on the Activities of Launching, Flight Operation or Guidance of Space Objects.
19. Finland, Act on Space Activities, 63/2018.
20. Portugal, Decree-Law No. 16/2019 of January 22, 2019.

I. DRAFTING HISTORY

The question whether the legislation Law of Luxembourg should cover all space activities under its jurisdiction and control including space resources mission was debated during the legislative works. However, the incorporation of the 2017 Law on Space Resources into the new legal document might have led to reopening numerous questions that were successfully closed by its adoption in Parliament. Therefore, on balance there was a clear tendency to avoid opening the 2017 Law on Space Resources. Consequently, the general space law was drafted to cover all space activities under the jurisdiction of Luxembourg with the exemption of space resources missions, which remain regulated by the 2017 Law on Space Resources.

This approach could be observed already in the 2018 Draft Law on Space Activities. Its Article 1 postulated that the new Law should not apply to the missions on exploration and utilization of the space resources regulated by the Law of July 20, 2017 on Exploration and Utilization of Space Resources, with the exemption of Article 16 (national registry of space objects), Article 17 (UN Register) and Article 18 paragraph 2 (exemption from insurance tax) of the present Law. The Commentary to this Draft rightly noted that the 2017 Law represents a *lex specialis*, whereas the new document should serve as *lex generalis* and be applicable in all cases not covered by the 2017 Law on Space Resources.[21]

However, the idea of including space resources mission at least partly in the upcoming Law on Space Activities was not abandoned completely. In its Opinion of November 2018, the Chamber of Commerce noted that it "understands the need to clearly confirm the keeping in force the 2017 Law on Space Resources" and to avoid that the procedures for authorization space resources missions are replaced by procedures envisaged for other activities. However, the Chamber suggested including space resources missions within the scope of the new law and to add a provision that would exempt them from the general authorization procedure. The suggested outcome would then be an article stating that "the present Law applies to missions of exploration and use of space resources ... with the exemption of articles 5 to 15 (authorization) of the present Law."[22]

This suggestion and proposed provision were not reflected in the Draft. The coordinated text prepared by the Commission of Economy[23] repeated the provision of the original Draft by stating that the new Law does not apply to the space resources missions with exemption of Article 15 (national registry) and Article 16 (exemption from the insurance tax). Only the original Article 17 referred to by the 2018 text of Article 1 dealing with furnishing of information in the national registry to the UN Secretary General was deleted from the Draft on the initiative of the Conseil d'État. It described it as superfluous, because these obligations are sufficiently regulated by the 1975 Convention on Registration of Objects Launched into Outer Space.[24]

21. 2018 Draft Law on Space Activities, p. 1.
22. Avis de la Chambre de Commerce (November 19, 2018) 6-7.
23. Amendements parlementaires (July 20, 2020).
24. Avis du Conseil d'État (February 15, 2019) 16.

II. INTERPRETATION

The exemption of space resources missions from the 2018 Draft was a pragmatic decision to enable the regulation of space mining under the earlier law, which was perceived as urgent by operators and politicians and leaving time to elaborate the general Space Law. From a practical point of view, it would be more comfortable to have one compact document dealing with all space activities under the jurisdiction of Luxembourg. However, the Opinion of the Conseil d'État[25] contributed to the harmonization of both texts to such an extent that the differences between the two documents are negligible.

The user interpreting this provision and contemplating whether an envisaged activity should be authorized under the 2017 or 2020 Law can practically spare this time. The only substantial difference consists in the fact that the 2017 Law on Space Resources enumerates the legal form of the operators as a precondition for authorization (Article 4) whereas the 2020 Law leaves this aspect open. Both procedures are so strongly unified that the decision for one or another law practically cannot have any impact on the outcome of the authorization procedure.

III. EVALUATION

The regulation of a specific area of activity by one or more texts usually has political reasons and flows from an urgency to focus on one specific issue. If regulated by two normative acts, as in case of the 2017 Law on Space Resources and the 2020 Law on Space Activities of Luxembourg, a legislative issue can be their subsequent amendments. If the highly harmonized procedure of authorization should be preserved, also future amendments will have to be coordinated.

The separation of the regulation of space resources missions and other space activities is not a unique approach chosen by Luxembourg. Also, Japan decided to adopt a specific regulation devoted to space resources—the 2021 Space Resources Mining Act[26]—which specifies the rules of the general 2016 Space Activities Act.[27] In the UAE, space resources are subject of the authorization procedure regulated by the 2019 UAE FLRSS,[28] with work on a specific space resources legislation ongoing. In comparison, the US provisions on resources mining are only legalized in the 2015 US CSLCA and no specific regulatory scheme has yet been adopted.[29]

---

25. *Id.* at 8.
26. 2021 Japan Space Resources Law, *see* Tajiro Suzuki, "Japan: Legal Issues in Space Business in Japan—Volume 2," Baker Mackenzie (July 9, 2021).
27. Act on Launching of Spacecraft, etc., and Control of Spacecraft, Act No. 76 of 2016.
28. 2019 UAE FLRSS, Art. 18.
29. 2015 US CSLCA, Title IV.

Article 2 Definitions*

For the application of this Law the following should be understood:

1. **"space activity": any activity consisting in launching or attempting to launch one or more space objects into outer space or in controlling one or more space objects or in using them during a stay in outer space, including the return to Earth, as well as any other activity taking place in outer space for which the Grand Duchy of Luxembourg is likely to be held internationally liable;**
2. **"Liability Convention": the Convention on International Liability for Damage Caused by Space Objects done in London, Moscow and Washington on 29 March 1972;**
3. **"damage": any harm to persons, property, public health or the environment directly caused by a space object within the scope of a space activity, excluding the consequences of use of the signal emitted by that object for users;**
4. **"space object": any object launched or intended to be launched into outer space, the component parts of such object and its launch vehicle and parts thereof;**
5. **"operator": any person who, on his own behalf, carries out or undertakes any space activity, alone or jointly with others;**
6. **"qualifying holding": the holding in an operator, either directly or indirectly, of at least 10% of the capital or voting rights, or any other possibility of exercising considerable influence over the management of that operator;**
7. **"Space Treaty": Treaty on Principles Governing the Activities of States in the Exploration and Use of Outer Space, including the Moon and Other Celestial Bodies, done in London, Moscow and Washington on 27 January 1967.**

* P.J. Blount

I. DRAFTING HISTORY

Article 2 provides for definitions of the key terms used in the Law. The notion of "space activity" has been inspired by the indications contained in the UN General Assembly Resolution 68/74 titled "Recommendations on national legislation relevant to the peaceful exploration and use of outer space."[1] The Draft designed this notion to enable the State to regulate any space activity for which it may be held liable under its international obligations and, in particular, under the Liability Convention.[2] The initial idea was to refer to activities related to the launch or attempted launch of any object into outer space, as well as activities consisting in using an object in outer space by controlling it as, according to the authors of the Draft, space activities must be carried out for the operator's own account.[3] Therefore, the authors of the Draft considered that the activity of controlling a space object on behalf of someone else does not fall under the definition of space activity and that in such a case, it is the one who makes use of the object that remains the contractor of the space activity and not the one to whom he has delegated the control.[4]

They also explained that a customer who rented a satellite capacity from the operator is not considered as carrying out a space activity but that only the satellite operator is considered as performing the space activity and must therefore obtain an authorization.[5] The authors of the Draft also described that the notion of operator refers to the one who carries out a space activity "on his or her own account," even if that means with the assistance of a third party, in particular to control a space object.[6] Thereafter, the Chamber of Commerce suggested to add to the notion of "space activity" that "any activity consisting of launching or attempting to launch one or more objects into space ... as well as any other activity that takes place in outer space for which the Grand Duchy of Luxembourg is likely to be held internationally responsible under the international agreements mentioned in the Annex," in order to provide legal certainty and recommended to add an annex referring precisely to the texts mentioned in the Law.[7] The Commission of Economy subsequently inserted the words "on its own behalf" to the definition of space operator.[8]

For the same reason, with regard to the notion of "attempt to launch an object," the Chamber of Commerce considered it would be necessary to specify from which moment onwards a space activity should be considered as an attempt to launch a space object.[9] The Conseil d'État criticized the decision by the authors of the Draft to have inserted the words "for its own account" in the definition of "space activity," noting

1. UN Resolution (UN) 68/74: Recommendations on national legislation relevant to the peaceful exploration and use of outer space, para. 1.
2. Convention on International Liability for Damage Caused by Space Objects, entered into force on September 1, 1972, 24 U.S.T. 2389, 961, U.N.T.S. 187.
3. 2018 Draft Law on Space Activities, Commentaire des articles, p. 11.
4. *Id.*
5. *Id.*
6. *Id.*
7. Notice from the Chambre de Commerce (November 19, 2018) 7.
8. Amendements parlementaires (July 20, 2020) 3.
9. *Id.*

that it would have been more relevant to see these terms inserted in the definition of "operator," since it is to this notion that the said precision applies.[10] The Conseil d'État added that the Draft Law should specify whether, if the space activity is carried out jointly by several persons, they will all be considered as "operator," especially in the case of a lease.[11]

The authors of the Draft modeled the definition of "space object" on that of Article 1(d) of the Liability Convention, including payloads attached to a satellite, and they took the definition of "damage" verbatim from Article I (a) of the Liability Convention.[12] The Conseil d'État noted that the definition of "damage" contained in the 2008 French Space Act[13] also refers to "environmental damage," which specified that the damage must have been caused directly by a space object in the course of a space activity and reminded that the French legislator excluded from this definition the consequences of the use of the signal emitted by the space object for the users.[14] Additionally, the Conseil d'État noted that the term "damage" is used only in the context of Article 12, paragraph 5, of the Draft Law.[15] Taking into account the observations of the Conseil, the Commission of Economy amended the definition of "damage" to model it on that provided for in Article 1, point 1°, of the 2008 French Space Act.[16]

However, the Chamber of Commerce noted that even though the term "damage" has been defined, no provision of the Draft refers to it thereafter, and that on the contrary, the notion of "launching State" is not defined, although it would allow the scope of application of the Draft set out in Article 1 to be expressed more precisely.[17]

The definition of "qualified participation" used in Article 2 corresponds to the definition provided in Article 1(25) of the 1993 Law on Financial Sector.[18] For the determination of the level of shareholding considered as "qualified," which is set at 10% of the capital or voting rights, the text refers, as does the aforementioned law on the financial sector, to the Law of January 11, 2008 on the Transparency Obligations of Issuers.[19] It should be noted, however, that the Draft also refers in Article 13 to a higher threshold of 20% which entails specific obligations.[20] The authors of the Draft underlined that this 10% threshold used to define a qualifying holding must be understood as a floor threshold, which does not exclude that qualifying holdings reaching a higher threshold may in turn serve as a criterion for the application of specific provisions.[21] The Conseil d'État proposed to replace the term "undertaking"

10. Avis du Conseil d'État (February 15, 2019) 2.
11. *Id.*
12. 2018 Draft Law on Space Activities, Commentaire des articles, p. 11, and Liability Convention, Art. I.
13. Loi française No 2008-518 du 3 juin 2018 relative aux opérations spatiales.
14. Avis du Conseil d'État (February 15, 2019) 2 and 2008 French Space Act, Art. 1(1).
15. Avis du Conseil d'État (February 15, 2019) 2.
16. Amendements parlementaires (July 20, 2020) 3.
17. *Id.*
18. Loi du 5 avril 1993 relative au secteur financier telle qu'elle a été modifiée, Art. 1(25).
19. Law of January 11, 2008 (coordinated version) on Transparency Requirements for Issuers, Art. 8.
20. No 7317, Commentaire des articles, p. 11.
21. *Id.*

with "operator," since it is the qualified participation in the capital of an operator that is referred to in Article 13 of the Draft Law on Space Activities.[22] The Commission of Economics followed the Opinion of the Conseil d'État, replacing the term "undertaking" with "operator"[23] and aligned the definition with that provided by Article 1(34) of the Amended Law of November 10, 2009 on Payment Services,[24] which refers to Article 4, paragraph 1, point 36, of Regulation (EU) 575/2013 on "qualifying holding."[25] Therefore, the definition became "the holding in an undertaking, directly or indirectly, of at least 10% of the capital or voting rights, or any other possibility of exercising a significant influence on the management of that undertaking."[26]

II. INTERPRETATION

This Article serves the very straightforward purpose of defining some of the terms used in the Law. The Article defines the following different terms.

Space Activity: The first definition is for the term "space activity," which serves a fundamental role in the Law as space activities are the *core foci* of the Law as the threshold that necessitates an authorization under the Law. The definition encompasses a number of activities: launch and attempted launch of space objects; controlling space objects (i.e., ground operations); the "use" of space objects "during a stay in outer space"; reentry of space objects; and other activities in space for which Luxembourg could be held "internationally liable." Space activities are, therefore, activities that interface—through launch, reentry, control, or use—with space objects.

Some of these activities are relatively clear, whereas others contain a great deal of ambiguity. There is likely little dispute over what constitutes launch operations, ground control operations, and reentry of space objects.[27] There is significantly less clarity in the use of a space object and other activities that could trigger Luxembourgish liability. Each of these will be addressed in turn.

Launch or Attempted Launch: Launch is core space activity. It is the act of placing an object into orbit via a launch vehicle. Most States with space laws regulate launch activities under their jurisdiction. For geographic reasons, Luxembourg is unlikely to launch from its territory, but like other States, Luxembourg has extended its jurisdiction in personam and requires authorization when its nationals are engaged in launch activities. The inclusion of "attempted launches" is important as it makes clear that even if the object fails to achieve intended orbital or suborbital trajectory, the attempt itself constitutes a space activity.

Controlling Space Objects: Controlling space objects refers to the command-and-control operations that happen from ground stations and terminals. Command and

22. *Supra* note 10, p. 2.
23. *Supra* note 8, p. 3.
24. Law of November 10, 2009 on payment services, Art. 1(34).
25. Regulation (EU) No. 575/2013 of the European Parliament and of the Council of June 26, 2013 on prudential requirements for credit institutions and investment firms and amending Regulation (EU) No. 648/2012, Art. 4.
26. *Supra* note 8, p. 3.
27. *See generally* Henry R. Herzfeld (ed.), A Guide to Space Law Terms (Space Policy Institute 2012).

control are different from other operations such as receiving data from the satellite, and concern primarily the ability to manipulate the satellite while in orbit. Ground operations can and do happen from Luxembourgish territory, but again the Law is extended in personam, so would also apply to extraterritorial control of the satellite.

The "use" of space objects "during a stay in outer space": The use of a space object also constitutes a space activity, but this phrase is particularly vague. In context, this likely means that when an organization employs a space object for its capabilities that it is engaging in a space activity. For instance, tasking a remote sensing satellite and receiving the data from that satellite's downlink could be considered a space activity as a use of a space object. This phrase becomes less clear when applied to space systems that allow end users to interact directly with the satellite. In the case of communications satellites that allow users to link directly to the satellite, it is unclear where the line is drawn between a use that constitutes a space activity and use that does not. An example would be the case of a satellite providing direct to home broadband services. In this scenario the end user is directly "using" the satellite for its capability, but such use would seem to fall outside the scope of activities requiring authorization. This provision could be clarified in the future regulatory framework.

Reentry of Space Objects: Some space objects are intended to reenter the Earth's atmosphere, either as an end-of-life procedure or as a planned return to the surface of the Earth. Reentry operations require an authorization for the same reasons that launch activities do, namely the danger posed to human life and property on the surface of the Earth.

Other activities in space for which Luxembourg could be held "internationally liable": The mitigation of State liability is one of the core themes under Luxembourg law. This phrase serves as a catch-all for activities that fall outside the scope of the listed activities but within the scope of the Article VII of the OST and the Liability Convention and is discussed in more detail in relation to Article 4 of the 2020 Law.

Liability Convention: This definition clarifies that Liability Convention is used to indicate the 1972 Convention on International Liability for Damage Caused by Space Objects. Luxembourg is a Party to the Liability Convention, and the international liability concerns seem to be a core driver in the adoption of the Luxembourg law.

Damage: The definition of damage is interesting in that it goes beyond the definition in the Liability Convention, which only includes harms done to persons or property (Article I). The definition adopted herein includes harm done to persons or property, and also extends to harm done to public health or the environment. This more expansive definition indicates that the concern is not just with liability originating within the bounds of international space law, but liability that may originate within other sources of law, including domestic law. Of particular note here is the inclusion of the environment. Damage to the environment would seemingly include damage done to the terrestrial, marine, or air environment, but it is unclear to what extent it would apply to the space environment and whether the creation of space debris could be an environmental damage.

This definition requires that the damage be "directly caused" by a space object. This means that there must be a direct nexus between the space object and the damage caused. Again, this differs from the text of the Liability Convention, which indicates that damage must be caused "by a space object" (Articles II-III). The language used in the 2020 Law on Space Activities may eliminate theories based on "proximate causation," which look beyond direct causation. While this formulation may not require a physical impact of a space object to cause damage, the definition excludes "consequences of use of the signal emitted by that object for users." As a result, data flows coming from space objects cannot cause damage as defined in the scope of the Law. This is notable as this type of damage has been discussed often in the context of the OST and the Liability Convention with no consensus on the bounds of causation under these instruments being reached.

Space Object: The concept of a space object is critical in international space law and in particular to the liability regime, which, as already noted, is directed at damage done by a space object. Despite this term's criticality in the space law regime, it is defined vaguely in the treaty texts. Specifically, the Liability Convention states that "[t]her term 'space object' includes component parts of a space object as well as its launch vehicle and parts thereof" (Article I). This definition fails to describe what constitutes the core definition of "space object" and instead focuses on ancillary items with a nexus to the space object, namely the launch vehicle and the component parts of the space object. The definition adopted in the 2020 Luxembourg law includes these items, but it also defines the substance of "space object" as "any object launched or intended to be launched into outer space." Thus, for the purposes of the Luxembourg law, a space object includes all physical objects that a space operator launches or attempts to have launched into space.

Operator: The definition of operator is contingent upon the definition of space activities. The space operator is anyone, whether an individual or a corporate entity that engages in space activities. Under the Luxembourg law, one of the core licensing considerations will be the appropriateness of the space operator for engaging in the space activities.

Qualifying Holding: While an operator may be an individual according to the 2020 Law on Space Activities, most likely these activities will be undertaken by an entity in a corporate form. As, noted elsewhere in this Commentary, the financial laws of Luxembourg have been a substantive inspiration in the drafting of the space laws. The qualified holding represents the threshold at which an entity has a substantive influence over the operator. This can be an entity holding either 10% of the capital or voting rights. Additionally, a qualifying holding can be manifested in a "possibility or exercising considerable influence" over the operator.

Space Treaty: This term refers to the 1967 Treaty on Principles Governing the Activities of States in the Exploration and Use of Outer Space, including the Moon and Other Celestial Bodies.

III. EVALUATION

The definitions adopted in Article 2 cover many of the most important definitional issues in regulating space activities, namely "space activity," "space object," and "damage." Providing definitions in a law is a balancing act. On one hand, if the definitions section describes the meanings of numerous terms, there is a risk of writing too much rigidity into the Law. On the other hand, if the definitions section fails to supply adequate meanings for certain terms, then there is a risk that the statute's application will be unclear and unpredictable. Striking this balance is particularly important in the current context of space development in which technological development can render laws obsolete. For instance, the term "launch," which is not defined in the Luxembourg law, could come under pressure through a restrictive definition as new methods of deploying space objects are adopted, such as the hand launch of a smallsat from a space station.

While the definitions adopted in the 2020 Law might not be comprehensive in their scope, they do tend to cut toward issues of applicability of the Law. Only time (and more specifically technological development during that time) will allow it to be seen whether these definitions can maintain their serviceability into the future.

Article 3 International Obligations[*]

The authorized operator may only carry out a space activity in accordance with the conditions of its authorization and the international obligations of the Grand Duchy of Luxembourg.

I. DRAFTING HISTORY

Article 3 of the 2020 Law on Space Activities appeared for the first time already in the 2018 Draft Law on Space Activities. Through the legislative process, this Article has undergone significant changes pursuant to the formal opposition expressed by the Conseil d'État in its Opinion of February 15, 2019.[1] Interestingly, the Chamber of Commerce did not make any comment on Article 3.

The original text of the Article read as follows: "All space activities shall be conducted in accordance with international law, including the Charter of the United Nations, with the goal of maintaining international peace and security and of promoting international cooperation and understanding. They will have to be conducted in compliance with the Outer Space Treaty as well as the other treaties and agreements to whom the Grand Duchy of Luxembourg is a Party."[2]

As one can easily notice, this first sentence is a *verbatim* transposition of Article III of the OST, which establishes the applicability of international law to space activities. The second sentence of the Draft of Article 3 explicitly reiterates compliance with the OST as well as other applicable treaties and agreements of which Luxembourg is a Party.

In its Opinion of February 15, 2019, the Conseil formally opposed this Article and demanded its suppression on the grounds that the obligations established in the

* Antonino Salmeri

1. Avis du Conseil d'État (February 15, 2019).
2. In French : "Toute activité spatiale doit être réalisée conformément au droit international, y compris la Charte des Nations Unies, en vue de maintenir la paix et la sécurité internationales et de favoriser la coopération et la compréhension internationales. Elle doit être menée en accord avec le Traité de l'Espace et les autres traités et accords auxquels le Grand-Duché de Luxembourg est partie." 2018 Draft Law on Space Activities.

provision can only be borne by a State and not by private operators.[3] The Conseil spotted the reference to Article III OST and interpreted it as an attempt to transfer Luxembourg's international obligations under that provision to private actors. In this respect, the Conseil argued that if a private space activity would violate international law, the Grand Duchy of Luxembourg would be the sole entity responsible for it. According to the Conseil, the State would not be able to escape its international responsibility by claiming that the relevant operator breached its obligations under the national space law. Notably, in motivating this response the Conseil referred to its previous Opinion of April 7, 2017 concerning the Draft Law on Space Resources, where it also expressed similar considerations.[4] As anticipated, the Conseil strongly opposed the imposition upon a private operator of the obligation to "maintain international peace and security and promote international cooperation and understanding" on the grounds that the latter can exclusively be borne by a State. Since a violation of this obligation could have been sanctioned under (the former) Article 14 of the Law with administrative fines, the Conseil formally opposed Article 3 in its entirety and demanded its suppression.

On July 20, 2020, the Commission of Economy approved several amendments to the 2018 Draft Law on Space Resources.[5] Notwithstanding the Opinion of the Conseil, the Commission found prudent that Article 3 would still include a reference to the international obligations of Luxembourg.[6] To address the concerns expressed by the Conseil, the Commission decided to rephrase Article 3 based upon the wording used for Article 2 of the 2017 Law on Space Resources. This change reflects the current text of the provision and was accepted by the Conseil in its second Opinion of September 29, 2020.[7]

II. INTERPRETATION

The purpose of Article 3 is to ensure that the space activities authorized by Luxembourg are conducted in compliance with relevant legal requirements of national and international law. To this end, Article 3 obliges operators to conduct their space activities in accordance with the conditions of their authorization and the international obligations of Luxembourg.[8] This provision is connected with Articles 5-10 of the 2020 Law on Space Activities, which establish the relevant authorization procedure, and Article 11, which provides the internal legal basis for the supervision powers of the competent Minister.

Under international space law, Article 3 implements the international obligations of Luxembourg as a Party to the OST and in particular those stemming from its Article VI. According to this provision, private activities in outer space shall require the

3. Avis du Conseil d'État (February 15, 2019) 3.
4. Avis du Conseil d'État (April 7, 2017).
5. Amendements parlementaires (July 20, 2020).
6. *Id.* at 4.
7. Avis complémentaire du Conseil d'État (September 29, 2020).
8. 2020 Law on Space Activities, Art. 3.

authorization and continuing supervision of an appropriate State, which shall assure their conformity with the provisions of the Treaty.[9] It is important to note that under Article VI of the OST these obligations are guaranteed by the international responsibility of the State concerned,[10] which means that their violation would constitute an internationally wrongful act.[11] Accordingly, through Article 3 of the 2020 Law on Space Activities, Luxembourg established the necessary internal legal basis to ensure that its private space activities are carried out in conformity with the provisions of the OST.

Notwithstanding the arguments put forward by the Conseil, it should be noted that pursuant to Article 3 the applicable international obligations of Luxembourg became legally relevant for private operators conducting space activities.[12] Since Article 3 connects the valid conduct of the authorized space activities with the respect of Luxembourg's international obligations, their potential violation by private operators would also entail a breach of Article 3. Consequently, the operator may be fined under Article 14 and could also be obliged to indemnify the Grand Duchy of Luxembourg in case the latter had to repair or compensate any damage caused.

III. EVALUATION

Article 3 of the Law on Space Activities is in line with other comparable provisions of national space legislation. For instance, this provision is very similar to Article 4(3) of the 2005 Belgian Space Law, according to which "space activities must be carried out in accordance with international law and, in particular, with the principles laid down in the Outer Space Treaty and the other treaties and agreements to which Belgium is a party."[13] Even more broadly, Article 9 of the 2019 Portuguese Space Law[14] obliges the license holder to "comply with and abide by international principles for the use of space, notably pursuant to the space treaties binding on the Portuguese Republic, including with relation to peaceful use, security and minimization of space debris."[15] Within the 2008 French Space Act, Article 5 provides that authorization requirements may be set forth "to ensure the respect by France of its international commitments." In the UK, Article 8(2) of the 2018 UK Space Industry Act establishes that the regulator can grant a license "only if satisfied that doing so is consistent with the international obligations of the United Kingdom."[16] Similar rules are also laid down in section 3 of

9. Outer Space Treaty, Art. VI.
10. *Id.*
11. Under the Articles on State Responsibility for Internationally Wrongful Acts. Resolution 56/83, adopted by the General Assembly at its 56th Session on December 21, 2001, Responsibility of States for Internationally Wrongful Acts. The consolidated text as adopted by UNGA Resolution 56/83 and corrected by UN DOC A/56/49(Vol. I)/Corr.4 is available online (accessed June 2021).
12. Through a mechanism known in public international law as "transformation." Alina Kaczorowska-Ireland, *Public International Law* (5th ed. 2015) 125.
13. *Id.* at Art. 4(3).
14. Decreto-Lei nº 16/2019 de 22 de Janeiro, Diário da República, 1.ª série—N.º 15—22 de janeiro de 2019.
15. *Id.* at Art. 9.
16. 2018 UK Space Industries Act, Art. 8(2).

the 2006 Netherlands Space Activities Law. From the above comparison, we can conclude that compliance with international law and the OST is especially important to all countries conducting or regulating space activities.

Article 4 Liability for Damage*

An operator that has obtained authorization for a space activity shall be fully liable for any damage caused during its space activity, including during any preparation works and duties.

I. DRAFTING HISTORY

Article 4 of the 2020 Law on Space Activities,[1] as adopted, was not originally included in the 2018 Draft Law on Space Activities. Initially, Draft Article 4 focused on limiting the environmental impact of space activities in outer space and on Earth.[2] It read: "An operator shall adopt necessary measures to limit the harmful degradation of the terrestrial and extra-terrestrial environments or their contamination as well as space debris risks." The environmental input in the Law was particularly welcomed by the Chamber of Commerce, which stressed the importance of sustainability in space.[3]

The Conseil d'État also welcomed the idea of including an environmental element in the Law and stressed that environmental protection is essential.[4] However, it regretted the vague phrasing of the original provision regarding the limitation of risks. It noted that the obligation to adopt measures was an obligation of means rather than of results, since all space activities are bound to create some damage to the environment. The Conseil d'État further raised the question of a potential violation of Draft Article 4, which should not require the realization of prior damage to the environment.

It suggested that damage to the environment be added to the definition of "damage" under Article 2 of the Law. As a result, the Commission of Economy[5] concluded that the added value of the original provision was questionable and noted

* Gabrielle Leterre
1. 2020 Law on Space Activities, Art. 4.
2. 2018 Draft Law on Space Activities, Art. 4.
3. Avis de la Chambre de Commerce (November 19, 2018) 7.
4. Avis du Conseil d'État (February 15, 2019) 3.
5. Rapport de la Commission de l'Economie, de la Protection des Consommateurs et de l'Espace (December 2, 2020) 4-5.

that it had no equivalent in the Law on Space Resources of 2017.[6] Thus, it decided to remove the Draft Article 4 and replace it with a provision similar to Article 16 of the Law on Space Resources.[7] Nonetheless, the Commission followed the Conseil d'État and implemented the suggested changes in Article 2 relating to the definition of "damage."

II. INTERPRETATION

Article 4, as adopted, is aligned with Article 16 of the 2017 Law on Space Resources, and it reaffirms that operators are liable for the damage they cause while carrying out the space activity defined in their mission authorization.[8] A notable difference with Article 16 of the 2017 Law, however, is the inclusion in Article 2 in the Law of a definition for the term "damage." Accordingly, "damage" encompasses "any harm to persons, property, public health or the environment directly caused by a space object within the scope of a space activity, excluding the consequences of use of the signal emitted by that object for users."

The inclusion of the environment in the list of damages for which operators can be held liable partially makes up for the loss of the strong environmental provision in the adopted text. In particular, "damage to the environment" could be interpreted in light of Draft Article 4, which referred to the degradation and contamination of the Earth and the outer environments as well as space debris. Accordingly, operators could be held liable, pursuant to Article 4, for damaging the terrestrial or extraterrestrial environments, notably by causing their harmful degradation, their contamination or by leaving space debris unattended.

III. EVALUATION

As noted in the Commentary of Article 16 of the 2017 Law on Space Resources,[9] Article 4 of the 2020 Law on Space Activities is analogue to the French and Belgian space legislations to the extent that it implies that the State may turn to the operator to bear the financial consequences arising from the occurrence of a damage while undertaking the space activity.[10] However, it can be noted that—contrary to France[11]—the Laws of

6. 2017 Law on Space Resources.
7. Article 16 of the 2017 Law on Space Resources states:

> The operator that is granted an authorization for a mission is fully responsible for any damage caused at the occasion of the mission, including at the occasion of all preparatory works and duties.

8. *See* the commentary in this volume on Art. 16 of the 2017 Law on Space Resources for an extended analysis.
9. *Id.*
10. 2005 Belgian Space Law, Art. 15; 2008 French Space Act, Art. 13.
11. In France, for instance, space operators' liability is limited to EUR 60 million per launching. *See* Assemblée nationale, Projet de loi autorisant l'approbation de la déclaration relative à la phase d'exploitation des lanceurs Ariane, Vega et Soyouz au Centre spatial guyanais, N° 3596 rectifié, 25 novembre 2020, pp. 9-10, 29-30.

2017 and 2020 of Luxembourg do not foresee a cap for the liability of operators. Nonetheless, the Law of 2020 fills some of the gaps left by the Law of 2017 by providing *inter alia* a definition for the term "damage."

Article 5 Ministerial Order*

(1) No operator can exercise any space activity without being previously authorized by the Minister in charge of the space policy and legislation, hereinafter the "Minister".
(2) Obtaining the authorization referred to in paragraph 1 shall not exempt the operator from the need to obtain other approvals or authorizations required.
(3) Any authorization to carry out space activity shall take the form of a ministerial order and shall be granted on written application sent to the Minister.
(4) For each application for authorization, a fee shall be fixed by the Minister to cover the administrative costs incurred in dealing with the application. This fee shall vary between 5.000 euros and 500.000 euros depending on the complexity of the application and the volume of work.
A Grand-Ducal regulation shall determine the procedure applicable for collection of the fee.
(5) Authorization shall be personal and non-assignable, subject to Article 12.

I. DRAFTING HISTORY

In the Commentary on Article 5, the authors of the 2018 Draft Law on Space Activities noted that the Luxembourg State is obliged under Article VI of the OST to ensure that space activities under its jurisdiction are carried out in accordance with the rules set out in that Treaty and must therefore set up a system for the authorization and supervision of such space activities.[1] They based the wording of Article 5 on the existing authorization and supervision provisions drafted for other regulated activities, in particular on the 1993 Law on the Financial Sector,[2] adapting them to the specific purpose of space activities and the concrete aim of the authorization and supervision

* Laetitia Zarkan and P.J. Blount
1. 2018 Draft Law on Space Activities, Commentaire des articles, p. 13, and Outer Space Treaty, Art. VI.
2. 1993 Law on the Financial Sector, Art. 2.

system.[3] They underlined that these provisions "borrowed" from other legal documents can be used as elements of interpretation of the general Space Law.

With regard to the need for authorizing space activities, the Chamber of Commerce stressed not only the importance of considering the potential impact of space activities on the Earth and in space but also the fact that the slightest drift in the exercise of this type of activity is likely to entail the moral and financial responsibility of the Luxembourg State, and could irremediably damage the image of the country on the international scene.[4] In its Opinion, the Chamber reminded that two types of administrative authorizations prior to the exercise of space activities were needed according to the original wording of the 2018 Draft: an authorization for the exercise of a space activity by an operator, and an authorization prior to any launch.[5] However, the Chamber noted that "the distinction between the two types of authorizations is not as simple as it seems" and underlined the vagueness of the provision as drafted.[6] Concerning "other approvals or authorizations" the operators are expected to apply for, the Chamber noted that the commercial operators would need a business license (permit) according to the 2011 Law regulating Access to the Professions of Craftsman, Trader, Industrialist and certain Liberal Professions.[7] It considered that the multiplication of authorizations and subsequently, of the competent administrative authorities, would add an administrative burden on companies.[8] On this topic of administrative burden, as for the form of the application for authorization, the Chamber recommended setting up a digital procedure of submission and authorization via a governmental site such as guichet.lu.[9]

In its 2019 Opinion, the Conseil d'État raised the question of whether—according to the 2018 Draft—it would be necessary to obtain a launch authorization for each space object, noting that the Commentary to the Draft Article 5 seemed to suggest so, but that there is no specific mention to such a requirement in the wording of the Article. If it would be the case, the provision should mention expressly that a launch authorization is requested "from an operator for any space object that it is preparing to launch into outer space." Furthermore, the Conseil d'État noted that if an operator has an authorization under Article 5, paragraph 1, and wishes to launch a space object, the operator to authorize would have to provide the competent Minister with the same information that it already gave for requesting an authorization to carry out a space activity.[10] The Conseil underlined the fact that the same reasoning applies when this operator intends to apply for an authorization under the 2017 Law on Space Resources.[11]

3. 2018 Draft Law on Space Activities, Commentaire des articles, p. 13.
4. *Id.* at 7.
5. Avis de la Chambre de Commerce (November 19, 2018) 7.
6. *Id.* at 8.
7. Law of September 2, 2011 regulating Access to the Professions of Craftsman, Trader, Industrialist and Certain Liberal Professions, Mémorial A N° 98, 22 septembre 2011, as amended.
8. Avis de la Chambre de Commerce (November 19, 2018) 8.
9. *Id.*
10. Avis du Conseil d'État (February 15, 2019) 3.
11. 2017 Law on Space Resources, Art. 13 and Avis du Conseil d'État (February 15, 2019) 3.

Concerning the necessity to obtain a business license, the Conseil d'État also questioned its appropriateness. Considering that the authorizations required in Article 5 make it possible to assess the professional experience and financial soundness of the operator, having to provide the same information to two different addresses under two different laws for the same purpose does not seem compatible with the concept of administrative simplification.[12] It added that institutions that are required to be licensed under the 1993 Law on the Financial Sector do not need such business license and referred to its Opinion of April 7, 2017, regarding Article 16 of Draft No. 7093,[13] which was to become the 2017 Law on Space Resources,[14] considering it was self-evident that the application for authorization can only be examined in the light of the conditions for granting authorization laid down in the Law.[15] In its observations of a legislative nature, using as a priority the nomenclature used in the Grand-Ducal Decree of January 28, 2015 on the Constitution of the Ministries, the Conseil d'État considered it would be important to avoid generic terms that could give rise to problems of interpretation at the time of a new distribution of governmental competences among the ministerial departments. Therefore, the Conseil d'État suggested that paragraph 1 should specifically refer to "the Minister responsible for spatial policy and legislation."[16]

During the session of the parliamentary Committee on Economics, Consumer Protection and Space, the Ministry representative confirmed that no other section of the bill distinguishes between two types of authorizations or establishes different or additional conditions for obtaining a specific launch authorization, and stated that such a distinction would be irrelevant.[17] Thereafter, the Committee decided to delete paragraph 2 on the launching authorization from the Draft Article 5 in its original wording[18] and instead adopt the wording of Article 17 of the 2017 Law on Space Resources.[19]

Concerning the collection of the filing fees provided for in paragraph 4 of the original wording of the Draft, the Chamber of Commerce noted that these fees could vary between EUR 2,000 and EUR 20,000, an amount that could be increased by the costs of an expert envisaged by the Draft, with the total not to exceed EUR 500,000. Comparing this fee with the one payable for obtaining a written mission authorization concerning the exploration or use of space resources under the 2017 Law on Space Resources, which varies between EUR 5,000 and EUR 500,000,[20] the Chamber suggested that the amounts of the various administrative authorizations relating to space

12. Avis du Conseil d'État (February 15, 2019) 3.
13. Opinion du Conseil d'État (April 7, 2017) 16.
14. 2017 Law on Space Resources, Art. 16.
15. Avis du Conseil d'État (February 15, 2019) 4.
16. *Id.* at 12.
17. Chambre des Députés, Commission de l'Economie, de la Protection des consommateurs et de l'Espace Procès-verbal de la réunion du 14 mai 2020, p. 6.
18. 2017 Law on Space Resources, Art. 17.
19. Chambre des Députés, Commission de l'Economie, de la Protection des consommateurs et de l'Espace Procès-verbal de la réunion du 14 mai 2020, p. 6.
20. 2017 Law on Space Resources, Art. 13.

activities be standardized so as not to create inequalities among operators[21] and regretted that an under-statutory norm dealing with the procedure for determining the amount of the fee could not be submitted together with the Draft. The final text of the Draft accepted the proposal of the Chamber of Commerce and aligned the fourchette of the fees with Article 13 of the 2017 Law on Space Resources.[22]

Concerning the nontransferability clause of the authorizations in Article 5, paragraph 5, the Chamber of Commerce reminded that the authorization allows the State, which is ultimately responsible, to control its risks by maintaining control over the evaluation of the technical, financial and "ethical" aptitudes of companies to operate in the space sector.[23]

II. INTERPRETATION

As explained in the preparatory works, the purpose of the 2020 Law on Space Activities is not only to authorize space activities but also to provide a legal basis for not authorizing them, when proper.[24] Luxembourg, as a Party to the OST, must "authorize" the activities of nongovernmental actors, and the ministerial order is the mechanism that the Grand Duchy has adopted to comply with this international obligation.[25] Without hindering the possibility for private individuals and legal persons to become operators, Luxembourg has to protect its interests and therefore, set up criteria for granting the authorization.

This provision begins with adopting the fundamental concept of a governmental authorization as a necessary prerequisite for engaging in space activities under Luxembourgish definitions. It does not, however, address what is necessary for an operator to gain an authorization leaving that information for later articles. It, rather, describes the nature and characteristics of the authorization itself. First, it can be noted that the provision does not identify which government minister will issue the authorization, instead simply noting that it will come from the Minister in charge of these activities. This gives a certain amount of flexibility to the government to rearrange its administrative competencies as needed. This Minister may set a fee between EUR 5,000 and EUR 500,000 for the processing of the authorization.

From an operator's standpoint, there are two important aspects of the authorization. First, the operator by gaining such an authorization does not exempt itself from other authorizations that may be needed, for instance a business license. Further, the ministerial order will be personal to the authorized entity and cannot be transferred or reassigned.

21. Avis de la Chambre de Commerce (November 19, 2018) 8.
22. Rapport de la Commission de l'Economie, de la Protection des Consommateurs et de l'Espace (December 2, 2020).
23. Avis de la Chambre de Commerce (November 19, 2018) 8.
24. 2018 Draft Law on Space Activities, Exposé des motifs, p. 3.
25. *Id*, at p. 4. *See also* Outer Space Treaty, Art. VI.

III. EVALUATION

In the first instance, two aspects of this provision stand out. First is the uncertainty in the fee. The difference between EUR 5,000 and EUR 500,000 is quite significant, and it is based on a ministerial determination as to the complexity of the authorizing process. This has potential to cause some entities to seek authorization in jurisdictions with more predictable fee structures. It is also notable that there is a floor for the fee and no ministerial discretion to waive the fee, which could have consequences for educational satellites. A second aspect is the no-transferability of the authorization except within the bounds of the provisions of Article 12. This could give pause to some operators that may wish in the future to sell their operations on to larger companies. The procedure envisaged in Article 12 for the transfer of space activities results in an entirely new authorization process.

The conditions required in Article 5 have been very similar to the ones of the 2005 Belgian Space Law[26] and the 2008 French Space Act[27] with regard to its personal and nonassignable nature and the method of delivering such an authorization. However, the 2005 Belgian Space Law emphasizes the importance for a space operator of complying with international law at any stage of the space operation.[28] Both the 2005 Belgian Space Law and the 2008 French Space Act also provide for any eventuality with regard to the interests of the safety of persons and property and the protection of public health and the environment.[29] Furthermore, the 2005 Belgian Space Law underlines the importance of safeguarding the environment; optimizing airspace and outer space use; and protecting Belgian strategic, economic, and financial interests.[30] The 2008 French Space Act highlights other aspects such as public health and environmental protection, emphasizing space debris and the protection of national defense interests.[31] According to the 2005 Belgian Space Law, the fees covering the administrative costs to be paid by the operator when submitting the application for authorization are determined by the King.[32] Additionally, the operator bears the costs of the technical experts,[33] as well as the fees related to the "incidence study."[34] The incidence study is the one carried out before an authorization is granted to assess the potential impact on the terrestrial environment or in outer space of the launch or operation of the space object.[35]

26. 2005 Belgian Space Law, Art. 11.
27. 2008 French Space Act, Art. 9.
28. 2005 Belgian Space Law, Art. 4.
29. 2005 Belgian Space Law, Art. 4; 2008 French Space Act, Art. 4.
30. 2005 Belgian Space Law, Art. 5.
31. 2008 French Space Act, Art. 4.
32. *Id.* at Art. 18.
33. *Id.*
34. *Id.* at Art. 8.
35. *Id.*

Article 6 Conditions of Authorization*

(1) An operator to be authorized shall provide evidence of the existence in the Grand Duchy of Luxembourg of its registered office and its central administration, including the administrative and accounting structure. An operator to be authorized shall have a robust system of financial, technical and legal procedures and methods by which space activity shall be planned and implemented. It shall also have a robust system of internal governance comprising in particular a clear organizational structure with well-defined, transparent and consistent lines of responsibilities, effective processes for the detection, management, control and reporting of risks to which it is or could be exposed, adequate internal control mechanisms, including sound administrative and accounting procedures as well as control and security mechanisms for its technical systems and applications.
The systems, processes, procedure and mechanisms referred to in the previous paragraph shall be exhaustive and adapted to the nature, scale and complexity of the risks inherent in the business model of the operator to be authorized as well as the space activity for which authorization is requested.
The members of the operator's governing body shall have the honourability, knowledge, skills and experience required to exercise their duties at all times. Honourability shall be assessed based on judicial records and all aspects able to establish that the persons referred to have professional honourability and present all the guarantees of irreproachable activity.
Any change in the persons referred to in the foregoing paragraph must be notified to the Minister in advance.
There must be at least two persons responsible for the management of the operator and they must be authorized to determine the direction of space activity effectively. They must have gained adequate professional experience by having already carried out similar activities with a high level of responsibility and independence in the space sector or a related sector.

---

* Laetitia Zarkan and P.J. Blount

(2) Authorization shall be subject to notification to the Minister of the identity of the shareholders or partners, whether direct or indirect, natural or legal persons, who have a qualifying holding, and of the amount of such holdings or, if the threshold provided for in Article 2, point 6, is not reached, of the identity of the twenty main shareholders or partners.
Authorization shall be refused if, taking into account the need to guarantee a sound and prudent operation, the capacity of the aforesaid shareholders or partners is not satisfactory.
The concept of sound and prudent operation shall be assessed in light of the following criteria:
1. the professional honourability of the operator to be authorized and of the shareholders and partners referred to in section 1;
2. the honourability, knowledge, skills and experience of every member of the governing body of the shareholders and partners referred to in section 1;
3. the financial soundness of the shareholders and partners referred to in section 1;
4. the existence of reasonable grounds for suspecting that a transaction involving or an attempt at money laundering or terrorist financing is in progress or has taken place in relation to the space activity envisaged or that such activity could increase the risk thereof.

The honourability of the members of the governing body of the shareholders or partners referred to in section 1 shall be assessed according to the terms of Article 6, paragraph 1, section 4, second sentence.
(3) Any change in the persons referred to in paragraph 1, section 4, must be notified to the Minister in advance. The Minister may request any information necessary on the persons that may be required to fulfil the legal conditions of professional honourability or experience. The Minister shall object to the change envisaged if such persons do not have adequate professional honourability or adequate professional experience or if there are demonstrable objective reasons for considering that the change envisaged risks jeopardizing a sound and prudent operation.
(4) Applications for authorization must be accompanied by an assessment of the risks of space activity. They shall specify the coverage of such risks by the operator's own financial resources, by an insurance policy arranged with an insurance company not belonging to the same group as the operator to be authorized or by a guarantee issued by a credit institution not belonging to the same group as the operator to be authorized.
Authorization shall be subject to the existence of financial bases appropriate to the risks associated with space activity.
(5) Authorization shall be subject to the condition that the operator to be authorized assigns the audit of its annual accounting documents to one or more approved auditors (*réviseurs d'entreprises agréés*) providing evidence of adequate professional experience.

Any change in the approved company auditors (*réviseurs d'entreprises agréés*) must be authorized by the Minister in advance.
The institution of commissaires who may form a supervisory board, provided for by the amended Law of 10 August 1915 on commercial companies, shall only apply to operators if required by the Law on commercial companies, even if there is a company auditor (*un réviseur d'entreprises*).

I. DRAFTING HISTORY

Based on the recommendations contained in the 2013 United Nations Resolution No. 68/74 on National Legislation Relevant to the Peaceful Exploration and Use of Outer Space,[1] Article 6 lists the conditions that the operator must meet in order to obtain an authorization and how such an application will be assessed by the Minister.[2] It has been underlined by the authors of the 2018 Draft that they intended to ensure, on the one hand, that the operator is able to respect the obligations under which it is authorized to carry out a space activity and, on the other hand, that the managers and shareholders or associates holding a qualified participation—at least 10% of the capital or voting rights—are trustworthy.[3]

The Chamber of Commerce noted that Article 6 aims in particular to protect the State, the citizens and the environment against possible risks that cannot yet be clearly identified because of the novelty of the space activities under development. Thus, the Chamber considered that a condition of acceptance would be the "respect of the rules of the art" and the "security of the persons and the goods and the safeguard of the environment."[4]

Concerning the notion of "operator" used in Article 6, the Commentary to the first version of the Law explained that the operator would constitute as a legal person under private or public law having its central administration and its registered office, including the administrative and accounting structure, on the territory of the Grand Duchy.[5] Thereafter, the representative of the Ministry of Economy suggested that the words "to be authorized" should be inserted after the first occurrence of the concept of operator, in the interests of drafting consistency with the 2017 Law on Space Resources.[6] The debate in the parliamentary Commission on Economy noted about this

1. UNGA Resolution 68/74: National Legislation Relevant to the Peaceful Exploration and Use of Outer Space, UN Doc. A/RES/68/74 (November 11, 2013).
2. 2018 Draft Law on Space Activities, Commentaire des articles, p. 14.
3. *Id.*
4. Avis de la Chambre de Commerce (November 19, 2018) 8.
5. 2018 Draft Law on Space Activities, p. 5.
6. Commission de l'Economie, de la Protection des consommateurs et de l'Espace, Procès-verbal de la réunion du 14 mai 2020, p. 8.

first paragraph, which requires the existence in Luxembourg of "a central administration and the registered office of the operator to be authorized, including the administrative and accounting structure," that the wording would be unusual and could cause problems in practice, as many companies prefer to outsource their accounting.[7] However, the representative of the Ministry of Economy justified this wording, explaining that given the great responsibility of the State that authorizes such activities, it was considered useful to ensure that the essential functions of such an operator are located on national territory. The political will would be to exclude that investors are tempted to establish "front companies" in Luxembourg and to ensure that key decisions are effectively taken in Luxembourg.[8] The representative added that the quoted wording does not exclude the use of third parties to perform the accounting work. In other words, it has been explained that the responsibility of the accounting established in Luxembourg must "imperatively" remain with the company, while outsourcing to specialized companies remains permitted.[9]

The authors of the Draft emphasized the importance for the operator to have a governance and risk management structure that is adequate for its space activities (Article 6 paragraph 2). The Chamber of Commerce commented about the provision on the notion of professional integrity and good repute of the operator and its governing body as formulated in paragraph 3 of the Draft Article 6 that the provision would grant a very broad discretionary power to the authorizing Minister, who alone decides whether to take a measure in one direction or another, among which is deciding whether or not to impose administrative penalties. According to its Opinion, the declaration of missing professional honorability values an administrative penalty.[10] The Chamber of Commerce declared that the provision was therefore likely to be contrary to the principle of the separation of powers guaranteed by the Constitution of the Grand Duchy of Luxembourg, and in particular to Article 49 thereof, which provides that "justice is administered in the name of the Grand Duke by the courts and tribunals."[11]The Chamber of Commerce affirmed that the executive power cannot have such a competence.[12] However, the provision remained unchanged.

Inspired by the 2011 Law regulating Access to the Professions of Craftsman, Trader, Industrialist and certain Liberal Professions,[13] the Chamber of Commerce also suggested that only a history not older than ten years should be used to determine a person's professional standing.[14] On this point, the Conseil d'État[15] wondered whether one would have to justify one's good character or one's professional character, or both,

7. Commission de l'Economie, de la Protection des consommateurs et de l'Espace Commission de l'Environnement, du Climat, de l'Energie et de l'Aménagement du territoire, Procès-verbal de la réunion du 28 mai 2020, p. 9.
8. *Id.*
9. *Id.*
10. Avis de la Chambre de Commerce (November 19, 2018) 8.
11. Constitution of the Grand Duchy of Luxembourg 1868, as amended to 2019, Art. 49.
12. Avis de la Chambre de Commerce (November 19, 2018) 8.
13. Law of September 2, 2011 regulating Access to the Professions of Craftsman, Trader, Industrialist and Certain Liberal Professions, Mémorial A N° 198 (September 22, 2011), as amended.
14. Avis de la Chambre de Commerce (November 19, 2018) 8.
15. Avis du Conseil d'État (February 15, 2019) 4.

on the mere basis of the criminal record, underlining that the wording of this provision was not clear on this subject, unlike Article 9 of the 2017 Law on Space Resources. Questions were raised about the control "of the necessary knowledge, skills and experience" carried out in practice, and a reference to the control methods of the Supervisory Commission active in the financial sector was discussed. The representative of the Ministry of Economy explained that in the area of space activities, this control is carried out according to the means available to the Luxembourg Space Agency (LSA), which still knows individually each company active in this sector. A specific procedure has not been put in place to control the competences of the members of the management body and is for the moment, taking into account the limited number of companies, not considered necessary.[16]

The first version of the Draft (Article 6(4)) required that the operator applying for authorization offers the moral, financial and technical guarantees to carry out these activities in compliance with the obligations imposed on it.[17] About this paragraph, the Conseil d'État asked what was a "moral guarantee" and whether—with regard to financial guarantees—[18] it would cover the same area as Article 10 of the 2017 Law on Space Resources. This provision was deleted from the text and replaced by a provision dealing with the insurance policy. This is commented in detail in the text related to Article 8 where the provision was originally included.

In paragraphs 5 and 6 of the original version of Article 6, the authors of the 2018 Draft intended to enable the State to assess whether the space activity would not harm public interests and considered that the State may refuse authorization in the event that authorization would expose it to risks of liability disproportionate to the benefits that the activities in question may represent for the State and its citizens.[19] The Chamber of Commerce approved this provision stating that "the space activity must not be of a nature to undermine public order and public security, to compromise the strategic, economic and financial interests of the Luxembourg State or the respect by the Luxembourg State of its international commitments."[20]

As for paragraph 5, the Conseil d'État declared that it agreed with the text but noted that the provision in question was not included in the 2017 Law on Space Resources. In its Opinion, the Conseil also formally opposed the original paragraph 6 allowing to refuse authorization in the event that authorization would expose the State to disproportionate risks of liability, on the grounds that the provision would be a source of legal uncertainty.[21] Wondering whether it would apply when a launch authorization is requested, Conseil d'État reminded that paragraph 6 required that the space activity to be authorized "must not expose the Luxembourg State to a disproportionate risk of international liability in relation to the interests that the space activity

16. Commission de l'Economie, de la Protection des consommateurs et de l'Espace ; Commission de l'Environnement, du Climat, de l'Energie et de l'Aménagement du territoire, Procès-verbal de la réunion du 28 mai 2020, p. 9.
17. 2018 Draft Law on Space Activities, p. 14.
18. Avis du Conseil d'État (February 15, 2019) 4.
19. 2018 Draft Space Activities Law, p. 14.
20. *Id.*
21. Avis du Conseil d'État (February 15, 2019) 4.

may represent for the Grand Duchy of Luxembourg."[22] In this context, the Conseil d'État wondered whether these "interests that the space activity may represent for the Grand Duchy of Luxembourg" would be moral (e.g., the notoriety given to Luxembourg) or material (e.g., the amount of taxes collected by the State).[23] Additionally, the Conseil d'État asked what is the "disproportionate" risk referred to and how should this condition be assessed, as well as which documents are to be provided by the applicant?[24] Consequently, these two provisions were deleted from the Draft.

A new point has been added to deal with the persons responsible for the management of the operator, in compliance with Article 9 of the 2017 Law on Space Resources.[25] This provision adds further conditions that the operator has to comply with to guarantee a sound and prudent operation of the space activity. The representative of the Ministry of Economy specified that this is one of the conditions that the operator must fulfill and takes into account the specificity of activities in outer space. This newly included Article 6 requires, i.e., that there must be at least two persons responsible for the management of the operator. Concerning this condition, the State wanted to guarantee that at every moment, at least one person would be present who is able to direct this activity or this space object, even in case of unexpected departures of people who have these crucial skills. The minimum condition of two persons with the same level of competence is intended also to guarantee that at each moment one person can replace the other person with regard to the concrete responsibility of the operational part of the space activity of the company.[26] This, however, did not imply that the authorization to carry out the respective space activity would be granted in the name of the persons in charge of the management of the operator. The authorization would be established in the name of the company that fulfills the listed conditions.[27]

II. INTERPRETATION

Article 6 lists the conditions that must be met to be granted an authorization to carry out space activities. This is an exhaustive list, and it serves as the basis for the Minister to deliver or deny the authorization. Keeping with the origins of Luxembourg space law in its banking and financial law, these requirements focus on the financial stability and corporate governance of the operator.

The first paragraph of the Article provides for an administrative obligation related to the place of establishment of the operator applying for authorization. The operator, in order to be authorized by Luxembourg, must show that both its registered office and its central administration are located in Luxembourg. The organization must demonstrate that it has a robust internal corporate governance process that encompasses

22. *Id.*
23. *Id.*
24. *Id.*
25. Commission de l'Economie, de la Protection des consommateurs et de l'Espace ; Commission de l'Environnement, du Climat, de l'Energie et de l'Aménagement du territoire, Procès-verbal de la réunion du 28 mai 2020, p. 10.
26. *Id.*
27. *Id.*

"financial, technical and legal procedures and methods" for managing the space activity undertaken and must specifically have governance processes that addresses risk assessment and management. The "systems, processes, procedure and mechanisms" identified in fulfillment of this requirement must be "exhaustive" and specifically "adapted to the nature, scale and complexity of the risks" associated with both the business model pursued by the applicant and the specific space activity envisioned. The individuals that are part of the governing body of the organization must show "honourability, knowledge, skills and experience required to exercise their duties" as proved by judicial records and other means. In addition to the governing body, at least two individuals must be tasked with managing the space activity and authorized to direct it. These two individuals must have previous experience in managing such activities either in the space sector or a related sector. Any changes to the governing board or the individuals tasked with management must be notified to the Ministry in due course. Section 3 of this provision notes that changes in the individuals tasked with managing the operation must be notified to the Ministry in advance.

The second section of this provision addresses the notion of "sound and prudent operation" of the space activity. This section first requires the applicant to disclose the identity of shareholders and partners in the organization that have a "qualifying holding" as defined in Article 2 of the Law. If there are no entities with a qualified holding, then up to 20 of the main shareholders or partners must be identified. Authorization must be denied if these shareholders or partners do not have the capacity to provide for a "sound and prudent" operation. This provision does not define "sound and prudent operation," instead gives a list of factors to be taken into account by the Ministry. These include the "professional honourability" of the operator and the shareholders; the "honourability, knowledge, skills and experience" of all members of the governing board of the shareholders; the "financial soundness" of the shareholders; and any potential for money laundering or financing of a terrorist organization through the enterprise. Honorability shall be determined using judicial records and other indicators as described in the first section of this provision.

As noted above, section 3 requires prenotification when the operations managers (addressed in section 1, paragraph 4) are to be changed. The Minister has a right to request the requisite information on the replacements and to reject the change if the suggested individuals do not have the adequate qualifications.

Section 4 requires that, as part of the application, the operator submit a risk assessment of the activity and proof of the financial resources to cover such risks. Such coverage can be from the operator's own financial resources, insurance coverage, or a guarantee from a credit institution. The latter two forms of coverage require that the institutions providing the coverage exist outside of the corporate group of the operator. Authorization requires that such coverage be adequate in light of the risks.

The final section of this provision covers the obligation for the operator to assign the audit of its annual accounting documents to approved auditors or commissaires.

III. EVALUATION

Inspired by the national legislation on the financial sector, the 2020 Law on Space Activities formulates in detail the conditions required of an operator. As a contrasting example, the 2008 French Space Act only provides for some rules related to the financial soundness of the operator, without more details.[28] According to the 2008 French Space Act, the financial guarantees should result from the written commitment of a credit institution, a finance company or an insurance company, a personal and joint guarantee, a first demand guarantee or liquid assets. Additionally, the operator shall send the Minister responsible for space a document proving the constitution of the financial guarantees before the start of the space operation.[29]

An interesting and significant difference is that the 2008 French Space Act specifies the technical requirements,[30] which is not the case of the Luxembourg Law. The 2020 Law on Space Activities does not make specific technical requirements mandatory. It instead relies on the two managers with previous experience in the space industry or a related industry. Indeed, this lack of technical requirements may be one of the most distinct features of the Luxembourg law. It is arguable that at least some technical aspects would be covered in the required risk assessment, but this places the burden on the company to identify the technical aspects rather than making positive obligations for compliance.

Another aspect of these requirements is that they place a high burden on the corporate governance aspects of the organization seeking authorization. This is related to the Law's goal of avoiding State liability but could potentially block some smaller or newer companies from access to authorization. While the governance processes and systems disclosed should be appropriate for the size of the undertaking, provisions such as the one requiring managers with previous experience in the space field, instead of the aforementioned compliance with technical requirements, could result in start-up companies seeking authorization in other jurisdictions.

28. Loi no 2008-518 du 3 juin 2008 relative aux opérations spatiales (2008 French Space Act), Art. 6.
29. Décret n° 2009-643 du 9 juin 2009 relatif aux autorisations délivrées en application de la loi n° 2008-518 du 3 juin 2008 relative aux opérations spatiales, Art. 16.
30. 2008 French Space Act, Art. 4.

Article 7 Useful Information*

Any application for authorization must be accompanied by all useful information for the assessment thereof as well as an activity programme. The standard content of an application for authorization may be established by a Grand-Ducal regulation.

I. DRAFTING HISTORY

Article 7 aims to describe the information that must be provided by the operator who applies for an authorization. Furthermore, the provision considers that a Grand-Ducal regulation may be the most fitting instrument to set the standard content of an application for authorization.[1] The role of such information is to enable the Minister to assess whether the conditions for obtaining an authorization, as *per* Article 5, are met.

The provision of Article 7 of the 2018 Draft Law on Space Activities was more complex. It required all "necessary" information to be submitted to the Minister. Additionally, it included the possibility to require from the operator an impact study related to legal, technological, and environmental risks, as well as an expert opinion on legal, technological, environmental, sanitary, and economic risks. In the latter case, the operator would have to give the experts access to the facilities and equipment it intends to use in the course of its space activity.[2]

The Chamber of Commerce criticized the lack of details framing the impact study and the request for a reasoned opinion from experts concerning the legal, technical, environmental, health, and economic risks that may result from the planned space activities.[3] It considered that the total absence of precision of the conditions for such requirement is likely to create a great deal of unpredictability for operators in the sector and invited the authors of the Draft to set out the criteria justifying the request for such information in the context of the authorization procedure to ensure a transparent and

* Laetitia Zarkan and P.J. Blount.
1. 2018 Draft Law on Space Activities, Commentaire des articles, p. 14.
2. *Id.*
3. Avis de la Chambre de Commerce (November 19, 2019) 9.

attractive legislative framework.[4] In its Opinion, the Conseil d'État noted that Article 6 of the 2017 Law on Space Resources refers to "useful information" instead of "necessary information," and to reach a consistency between the general Space Law and the 2017 Law on Space Resources, the Conseil proposed unify these terms.

Similar to the Chamber of Commerce, the Conseil discussed the requirement of an "impact study" and the "expert opinion" envisaged by the Draft, and highlighted the difference between these two terms. Hence, the Conseil d'État encouraged the authors of the Draft to make it more consistent with the 2017 Law on Space Resources.[5] Additionally, the Conseil suggested to remove the last sentence of the Article that obliged the experts to the professional secret, expressly sanctioned by the Luxembourg Criminal Code[6] as it underlined that Article 458 of the Criminal Code necessarily applies to experts.

Thereafter, the parliamentary Commission of Economy accepted the suggestions and modified the Draft.[7] The new text replaced the term "necessary" with "useful." It also removed the provision on the expert opinions. A Minister can always consult experts without a need for a specific legal provision to do so.[8] In the end, the final version of Article 7 only uses former paragraph 1 of the Draft law, which has become the sole provision of this Article.[9] With the intention of ensuring greater consistency between the provisions of the Draft and that of the 2017 Law on Space Resources, the Commission added a requirement for the provision of an "activity program" accompanying any application for authorization, instead of an impact study.[10]

II. INTERPRETATION

Article 7 requires that an application for authorization to carry out space activity includes "all useful information for assessment" of the application. It is unclear whether this means all useful information relating to the requirements enunciated in Article 6, which lays out the requirements for authorization, or whether this expands the scope of what must be provided. It specifically requires an "activity program" for the operations. This could be an important part of a risk assessment as required under Article 6, or a separate document containing strictly technical information. This provision also allows the authorizing Minister to make requirements as to the content of standard application via Grand-Ducal regulation.

4. *Id.*
5. Avis du Conseil d'État (February 15, 2019) 5.
6. Code pénal, 16 juin 1879, tel que modifié par Loi du 5 juin 2019, Mémorial A N° 397 du 12 juin 2019, p. 1.
7. Commission de l'Economie, de la Protection des consommateurs et de l'Espace, Procès-verbal de la réunion du 18 juin 2020, p. 2.
8. *Id.* at 9.
9. Rapport de la Commission de l'Economie, de la Protection des Consommateurs et de l'Espace (December 2, 2020) 9.
10. Commission de l'Economie, de la Protection des consommateurs et de l'Espace, Procès-verbal de la réunion du 18 juin 2020, p. 9.

III. EVALUATION

While the ambiguity in this provision could be problematic, this is mitigated by the ability of the Minister to formulate regulations specifying standard content in an application for authorization. Indeed, the critique of Article 6 and its potential to discourage start-up applicants could be mitigated through this regulatory process. Such regulation would not be able to derogate from the requirements of Article 6 but could potentially scale such disclosures appropriately for various types and sizes of entities. This is similar to the 2005 Belgian Space Law, which refers to sub-statutory rules. The 2005 Belgian Space Law does not give many details about the requirements an operator must meet to obtain an authorization and instead leaves these to Royal decree.[11]

11. 2005 Belgian Space Law, Art. 5.

Article 8 Further Specifications*

(1) The authorization shall describe the way in which the operator to be authorized satisfies the conditions of Articles 6 and 7. It may also contain provisions on:

1. **the activities having to be carried out in or from the territory of the Grand Duchy of Luxembourg;**
2. **the limits to which the space activity could be subject;**
3. **the procedure for supervision of space activity;**
4. **the conditions serving to ensure that the operator to be authorized fulfils its obligations.**

(2) The authorizations shall be subject to payment by the operator of an annual fee to the State. The annual fee shall be between 2,000 euros and 50,000 euros depending on the costs incurred by supervision, and it may be increased by experts' expenses incurred without being able to exceed 500,000 euros per annum. A Grand-Ducal regulation shall determine the procedure applicable for collecting the annual fee.

(3) The granting of authorization shall imply for the operator the obligation to notify the Minister voluntarily, in writing and in a complete, consistent and comprehensible manner of any substantial change in the information used by the Minister to examine the application for authorization.

I. DRAFTING HISTORY

Article 8 as formulated by the 2018 Draft Law on Space Activities was different from the final version. It required that the examination of the application must be carried out within six months. It allowed the Minister to add and to modify the conditions for an application for authorization and allowed the Minister to require an insurance of a space activity. Furthermore, the Article proclaimed that the authorization would be

* Laetitia Zarkan and P.J. Blount

accorded for a limited period of time. The only part which has remained unchanged related to the paragraph regulating the fee payable on an annual basis by the operator. One after another the provisions were contested mostly by the Conseil d'État, and they were finally substituted with a text which has been transposed from Article 12 of the 2017 Law on Space Resources. The commentary on the details of the new provisions can be found in the commentary in the present volume on the 2017 Law on Space Resources (Article 12).

Concerning the original six months deadline for authorization determined in Article 8, authors of the Draft considered that a period of six months would be necessary in certain cases to allow for the evaluation by experts of the risks that the space activity may entail and the measures that may be required to limit these risks.[1] The Chamber of Commerce questioned the six-month period, considering the administrative process would be too slow for the operators and could have a repulsive effect on the entrepreneurial dynamism in Luxembourg. The Chamber proposed to shorten this period and to make available to the applicant, upon receipt of the request, a graph that could be consulted online describing the different steps to be completed (by the administration as well as by the applicant) and the associated chronology until the final decision.[2] As the six-month period during which the Minister can take a decision should start after receipt of the "complete file," the Conseil d'État asked whether the application was considered as complete before or after receipt of the impact study or opinions of the experts envisaged by Article 7.[3] Because of the uncertainty this wording created, determining the deadline for a decision has been removed from the final version of the Article. Therefore, the ordinary legislation of Luxembourg will apply to the process.[4]

With regard to the actual authorization decision, the authors of the Draft stated that the content of the authorization could be modulated by the Minister according to the nature of the space activities and the risks they entail. Special conditions could be attached to the authorization and be adjusted over time in case circumstances change, to ensure compliance with the obligations imposed on the operator.[5] The Conseil d'État objected with the possibility for the Minister to attach to the authorization "any special conditions that he deems necessary to ensure compliance with the conditions" of the Law and the possibility the Minister has to modify these conditions in the event of a "change in the circumstances that governed the granting of the authorization require it." The Conseil d'État considered it a violation of Article 11, paragraph 6, of the Constitution of Grand Duchy of Luxembourg,[6] which guarantees the freedom of trade.[7] The Conseil affirmed that the conditions for the granting of a license must be set out in the Law and that it is not for the Minister to add to the Law conditions that are not set

1. 2018 Draft Law on Space Activities, Commentaire des articles.
2. Avis de la Chambre de Commerce (November 19, 2018) 9-10.
3. Avis du Conseil d'État (February 15, 2019) 5.
4. Amendements parlementaires (July 20, 2020) 10.
5. 2018 Draft Law on Space Activities, p. 14.
6. Constitution coordonnée du Grand-Duché de Luxembourg, Mémorial A N° 23, 22 octobre 1868, Art. 11.
7. Avis du Conseil d'État (February 15, 2019) 5.

out in it, but only to examine whether the conditions of Article 6 are fulfilled.[8] It also added that such a possibility does not exist in the 2017 Law on Space Resources.[9] Therefore, the Commission of Economy, preparing the final Draft, deleted this paragraph, considering it would have given arbitrary power to the competent Minister.[10]

Concerning the question of insurance which has been later included in Article 6(4) of the 2020 Law on Space Activities, the authors of the Draft gave the Minister a discretionary power to decide whether the operators have to conclude insurance covering both their own liability and the risks incurred by the State authorizing space activities. As explained in the Commentary to the 2018 Draft, Article 8 did not provide for a specific liability regime for operators for space activities, as is the case in certain foreign laws.[11] It was considered that the principles and rules of ordinary legislation on civil liability, as set out in the Civil Code,[12] are sufficient to regulate the conditions under which an operator may be held liable for his space activities both vis-à-vis third parties and, where applicable, vis-à-vis the Luxembourg State. Thus, in the event that the State is held civilly liable under the Liability Convention, the authors of the Draft explained that there will be a subrogation claim against the operator whose space activity is at issue on the basis of ordinary legislation.[13]

The Chamber of Commerce questioned the scope and consequences of the possibility granted to the Minister by the original Article 8 to require the operator to take out insurance covering the risks of liability incurred by either the operator or by the Grand Duchy of Luxembourg as a result of the authorized space activities. Considering that the objective announced in the Commentary on the Articles, is "to regulate the consequences of the international obligations arising for the operator from the space law," the Chamber pointed out that the obligation to take insurance is not consistent with the principles of the 1972 Liability Convention as it neither addresses the question of the liability of the actions carried out nor the extent of the required insurance coverage.[14] The Chamber of Commerce noted that Luxembourg alone has unlimited liability vis-à-vis third parties in the event of damage caused by the space activity for which it is considered to be the launching State[15] and that Article 8 of the Draft only provided for the possibility for the Minister to impose insurance coverage on an operator in the administrative authorization. The Chamber underlined the fact that the absence of a rule concerning the implementation of the operator's responsibility by the State at the national level in the event of the implementation of the State's international responsibility under the applicable international conventions would be likely to create legal uncertainty that is detrimental to both economic operators and the State.[16]

8. *Id.*
9. 2017 Law on Space Resources and Avis du Conseil d'État (February 15, 2019) 5.
10. Amendements parlementaires (July 20, 2020) 10.
11. Avis de la Chambre de Commerce (November 19, 2018) 15.
12. Code du 15 mars 1803—Code Civil.
13. 2018 Draft Law on Space Activities, p. 15.
14. Avis de la Chambre de Commerce (November 19, 2018) 10.
15. 1972 Liability Convention, Arts. II and III.
16. Avis de la Chambre de Commerce (November 19, 2018) 11.

In its Opinion, the Chamber of Commerce also stated that in the context of the administrative authorization of space activities, the extent of the State's liability vis-à-vis third parties does justify requiring the operator to take insurance to cover part of the State's liability.[17] It also expressed its concerns about the lack of a limit to the insurance cover required from the operator, considering that it would de facto make any space activity almost impossible in Luxembourg because of the difficulty of finding an insurance company prepared to cover the unlimited liability of the Luxembourg State.[18] Consequently, the Chamber suggested to provide for specific liability rules and to frame the requirements for insurance coverage of operators in the space sector in order to allow a controlled and coherent development of space activities in Luxembourg.[19]

In view of the risks inherent in space activities, the Conseil d'État wondered whether an insurance policy should not be made a condition of Article 6 instead of Article 8. Moreover, the Conseil d'État asked if this obligation, required at the time of delivery, was a suspensive condition to be granted with the authorization.[20] On this point, the Commission of Economy agreed with the Conseil d'État's suggestion and moved this paragraph from Article 8 to Article 6.[21] The provision on the liability of operators for damages caused during space activities has been regulated in Article 2 of the 2020 Law and is commented in relation to this provision.

Article 8 also provided that the authorization would be granted for a fixed period and that it may be renewed. Additionally, the Minister was initially planned to fix the amount the annual fee to be paid by operators, according to the actual surveillance costs, on the basis of a range.[22] The Chamber of Commerce approved the use of a range for determining the amount of the annual fee but requested for more information that would make it possible to determine this duration with regard to the mention to a "specified period." The Chamber invited the authors of the Draft to set out the period of validity envisaged in the form of objective criteria and conditions. However, it also questioned whether limiting the duration of the authorization would be relevant as each launch (by definition limited in time) seems to be subject to a separate authorization from the space activity itself, which is subject to regular controls and can be withdrawn or suspended if the operator no longer complies with the applicable conditions.[23] Thereafter, the Conseil d'État referred to its Opinion of April 7, 2017 on the Draft Law on Space Resources and formally objected to setting a fixed period for the authorization, on the grounds that: "the Article under consideration specifies neither the minimum nor the maximum duration of the approval. The Conseil d'État saw in the absence of such an indication a restriction on the freedom of trade guaranteed by Article 11(6) of the Constitution of Luxembourg."[24] The Commission of Economy

17. *Id.*
18. *Id.*
19. *Id.*
20. Avis du Conseil d'État (February 15, 2019) 5-6.
21. Amendements parlementaires (July 20, 2020).
22. 2018 Draft Law on Space Activities, p. 15.
23. Avis de la Chambre de Commerce (November 19, 2018) 9-10.
24. Avis du Conseil d'État (April 7, 2017).

agreed with the Opinion of the Conseil d'État and deleted several provisions of the original Article 8 and to ensure consistency with the 2017 Law on Space Resources, the content of Article 12 of the 2017 Law was inserted as a new paragraph 1 in this Article.[25]

II. INTERPRETATION

Article 8 addresses the contents of the authorization once it has been granted. The authorization itself must articulate how the authorized entities fulfill the requirements enumerated in Articles 6 and 7. Presumably, this articulation makes these ongoing requirements for maintaining the authorization. The authorization may also contain further provision for the authorized entity to comply with in the execution of the activity. These include specifying certain activities that must be carried out in the territory of Luxembourg, limitations to how the operator may carry out the activity, procedures for supervision of the activity, and other conditions that ensure the operator will comply with its obligations.

The second section imposes an annual fee payable to the State that ranges between EUR 2,000 and EUR 50,000. The fee is set based on expenses incurred in the supervision of the activity. This fee can be further increased based on expenses of experts employed in the supervision of the activity with a cap of EUR 500,000. A regulation should be promulgated on the collection of the fee.

The final section places a burden on the operator to inform the Ministry if any substantive changes have occurred in the information provided for the assessment of the authorization.

III. EVALUATION

This provision makes clear that the authorization can require compliance with more than just what is put for in the application for authorization. Indeed, this provision shifts from the international obligation to authorize and focuses on the obligation to "continually supervise" a space activity.[26] The additional requirements imposed here are not requirements for authorization, but rather requirements implemented through the authorization to comply with supervision.

It is also notable that the supervision of the activity is connected to a fee. This fee is interesting in that it is linked directly to costs incurred through the act of supervision. However, the divergence between EUR 2,000 and the potential of up to EUR 500,000 as an annual fee could have the effect of pushing operators to other jurisdictions, many of which do not impose ongoing supervision fees. The provision does include the potential for a regulation to address the fee, which could make its application more predictable.

---

25. Amendements parlementaires (July 20, 2020) 10.
26. Outer Space Treaty, Art. VI.

Article 9 Withdrawal of Authorization*

(1) Authorization shall be withdrawn if:
1. **the conditions for granting it are no longer fulfilled;**
2. **the authorization was obtained by means of false declarations or by any other irregular means;**
3. **the operator does not make use of it within a period of thirty-six months as from the granting thereof and abandons or has ceased to carry out its activity in the last six months.**

(2) In the event of the withdrawal of authorization, the Minister shall take all necessary measures to prevent the space activities for which the authorization was withdrawn from affecting the safety of persons or property or the environment or causing an increased risk of international liability for the Luxembourg State. The Minister may request the services of third parties for these purposes or transfer control over the space object to another operator to ensure the continuity of flight operations and guidance and, if necessary, to ensure re-orbiting or de-orbiting, even if such operations risk giving rise to the loss or destruction of the space object.

I. DRAFTING HISTORY

Through the legislative process, Article 9 of the 2020 Law on Space Activities has undergone significant changes pursuant to the series of formal opposition expressed by the Conseil d'État.[1] It first objected the inclusion of a suspension regime in addition to the possibility to withdraw the authorization. It noted that the Draft provision did not provide a regime to frame the suspension of authorization, nor did it indicate in which cases suspension would be chosen over withdrawal. The Conseil d'État further remarked that no period of suspension was indicated in the Draft; a point that was also

* Gabrielle Leterre
1. Avis du Conseil d'État (April 7, 2017) 6.

raised by the Chamber of Commerce.[2] Both entities considered that the lack of timeframe constitutes a risk toward legal certainty. The Conseil d'État further contested this point by arguing that suspension amounts to a sanction and that the provision should, thus, be precise pursuant to the principle of legality in criminal law. As a result, the Commission of Economy decided to remove the possibility for suspension of the mission authorization altogether.

Additionally, the Conseil d'État, in agreement with the Chamber of Commerce, further opposed the lack of specific timeframe in the Draft paragraph 1(3) regarding the possibility to withdraw the authorization in cases it is not made use thereof.[3] Accordingly, the Commission of Economy decided to align the period on Article 14 paragraph 2 of the 2017 Law on Space Resources and settled on a three-year period after which the authorization can be withdrawn if not used.

In addition, Article 9 used to provide, in a second paragraph, for the withdrawal or suspension of authorization on the ground of a "change of circumstances" compared to the initial situation that justified the delivery of the document. The Conseil d'État formally opposed the provision, arguing that its phrasing was too vague to provide legal certainty. It further noted that the 2017 Law did not offer similar restrictions. The Commission of Economy agreed with the assessment of the Conseil d'État and decided to remove the drafted paragraph 2 for purposes of harmonization with the 2017 Law on Space Resources.

II. INTERPRETATION

Similar to the 2017 Law on Space Resources,[4] the 2020 Law on Space Activities provides for the withdrawal of the operator's authorization to carry out activities in space in five cases. First, the operator violates its legal obligations under the authorization document or under the 2020 Law on Space Activities in particular and Luxembourgish law in general, as well as Luxembourg's international obligations, such as the ones under the ratified UN Space Treaties.[5] Second, the operator made false declarations, for instance, regarding the information they are required to share when requesting an authorization,[6] or misled the Minister into granting the authorization. Third, the operator abandoned its activity or—fourth—it "ceased to carry out [its]

2. Avis de la Chambre de Commerce (November 19, 2018) 11-12.
3. 2018 Draft Law on Space Activities, Art. 9 para. 1(4).
4. *See* 2017 Law on Space Resources, Art.14.
5. As of January 2021, Luxembourg is a Party to three of the five UN Space Treaties: the Treaty on Principles Governing the Activities of States in the Exploration and Use of Outer Space, Including the Moon and Other Celestial Bodies, entered into force on October 10, 1967, 610 U.N.T.S. 205 (Outer Space Treaty), the Convention on International Liability for Damage Caused by Space Objects, entered into force on October 9, 1973, 961 U.N.T.S. 187 (Liability Convention) and the Convention on Registration of Objects Launched into Outer Space, entered into force on September 15, 1976, 1023 U.N.T.S. 15 (Registration Convention). Luxembourg is also working on becoming a Party to the Agreement on the Rescue of Astronauts, the Return of Astronauts, and the Return of Objects Launched into Outer Space, entered into force on December 3, 1968, 672 U.N.T.S. 119 (Return and Rescue Agreement).
6. *See* 2017 Law on Space Resources, Arts. 7-12.

business" for the last six months, for instance due to the dissolution of the commercial entity. Last, the operator has not "made use" of the authorization during the first three years following its obtaining.[7]

Nonetheless, it is worthy to note that, in the 2017 Law on Space Resources, the legislator had not planned for cases when operators would abandon their activity. Rather, it offered operators the possibility to "renounce" to their authorization.[8] Though they have the same outcome—the decision of the operator leads to the withdrawal of the authorization—the focus between abandonment and renouncement shifts. In the first case, the focus is on the activity which is abandoned whereas in the second, it is on the administrative document. Furthermore, "abandonment" can refer to cases where operators are forced to stop their activity due to circumstances outside their control whereas "renouncement" is based on their willful action.

In addition, Article 9 of the 2020 Law on Space Activities introduces a new paragraph compared to the 2017 Law on Space Resources. Paragraph 2 tackles potential negative consequences resulting from the withdrawal of authorization and orders the Minister to adopt necessary measures in an effort to circumvent them. It foresees cases where the withdrawal would affect "the safety of persons or property or the environment" or "caus[e] an increased risk of international liability for the Luxembourg State." Paragraph 2 shows that Luxembourg is concerned about "the continuity of flight operations and guidance" and possibly the "re-orbiting or de-orbiting" of the space object. It aims to avoid collision with other space objects as well as the creation of space debris by leaving the space object unattended in outer space.

When losing their authorization to carry out activities in outer space, operators are forced to cease the activity. In some cases, as exemplified by paragraph 1, the termination of the activity is outside their control; in others, their violation of their legal obligations simply does not inspire trust in them. Nonetheless, no matter the circumstances, it remains that leaving a space object unattended in outer space can be dangerous, especially when considering that activities in outer space are naturally considered ultra-hazardous. Furthermore, pursuant to Article VI of the OST, Luxembourg must not only authorize but also continuously supervise space activities carried out by nongovernmental entities under its jurisdiction. Thus, it could be remiss in its obligations to not plan for such situation. For this reason, Luxembourg provides for the possibility to call on third parties that would be qualified to safely continue or terminate the activity.

III. EVALUATION

The legal grounds identified in Article 9 of the general Law on Space Activities for the withdrawal of authorization are in line with similar provisions found in foreign

7. *See* the commentary in this volume on the 2017 Law on Space Resources, Art. 14.
8. 2017 Law on Space Resources, Art. 14 para. 2.

national space legislations.[9] The deletion of the suspension regime, which coexisted with the possibility for the Minister to withdraw the authorization, is regrettable as it would have given operators a chance to modify their behavior before losing their authorization altogether. The formal opposition of the Conseil d'État over the possibility to suspend the authorization was not so much on the existence of a suspension as such than the lack of proper framework for it. Several other States have included the possibility for suspension in addition to withdrawal in their national space legislation.[10] However, the fact that a suspension regime does not exist is soften to an extent through the possibility to have a judge fine an operator until it complies with the Law. Article 14, paragraph 3 of the 2020 Law on Space Activities provides that a judge "may pronounce termination of the space activity contrary to the provision of this Law under a penalty of a fine ... per day of infringement." Thus, rather than withdraw the authorization entirely, operators can be compelled to fix their wrongdoings under the threat of a heavy fine and then go back to carrying out the space activity in compliance with the Law. As such, the sanction regime prescribed in Article 14 can be used to avoid disproportionate actions in cases where the suspension of the authorization would have been more favorable than its withdrawal. It balances, to an extent, the rigid regime of withdrawal prescribed in Article 9 of the 2020 Law, notably in cases where operators no longer fulfill the conditions set in the authorization, for reasons outside their control. However, it must be noted that the possibility to fine an operator until they comply with the Law lays with the judge whereas the decision to withdraw an authorization gives direct powers to the Minister to act.

Furthermore, while the Minister may appear to enjoy a wide margin of discretion in deciding to withdraw an operator's authorization to carry out space activities, it is not without its limits. It is always possible for an operator to appeal the Minister's decision in front of a judge. In Luxembourg, in particular, the State is held to the same standard as its private citizens.[11] As such, there is no specific condition or exception attached to the engagement of the Government's liability; general tort law applies and the administration can be held liable for a simple fault.[12] This particularity of the Luxembourgish legal system plays in favor of operators by ensuring it is not tremendously difficult to challenge the Minister's decision to withdraw the authorization. Conversely, France, for instance, operates under a hybrid system with distinct administrative and judicial "ordinary" jurisdictions reflected in distinct liability regimes for private citizens and its administration.[13] This distinction shines in cases where the

9. For example, 1993 South African Space Act, Art. 13; 2021 UK Space Industry Regulations, Art. 15; 2008 French Space Act, Art. 9; and Statute on Licensing Space Operations, No. 104, Art. 25 (1996) (RU).
10. For example, 1993 South African Space Act, Art. 13; 2021 UK Space Industry Regulations, Art. 15; and 2008 French Space Act, Art. 9.
11. Constitution du 17 octobre 1968, Mémorial A - 406 du 15 mai 2020, art. 84 (LU); Loi du 1er septembre 1988 relative à la responsabilité civile de l'Etat et des collectivités publiques, Mémorial A N° 51, art. 1(1) (LU).
12. G. Ravarani, *La responsabilité civile des personnes privées et publiques* (Pasicrisie luxembourgeoises 2020) paras. 8, 83-85.
13. This distinction of liability regimes between private and public entities was established in France by the Conseil d'État's decision in *Blanco* in 1873. The Court stated that "the liability which may

French administration will only be held liable for a "manifest error"—a threshold that does not exist for relations between private entities.[14]

Lastly, it can be noted that the allowance for the Minister to adopt necessary measures, including relying on third parties, to circumvent potential negative effects of withdrawing an authorization to carry out space activities also finds an equivalent in the 2005 Belgian Space Law.[15]

be incumbent on the State for damages caused to individuals, by the acts of the persons it employs in the public service, cannot be governed by the principles which are established in the Civil Code, for the relations between privates." Tribunal des conflits du Conseil d'État, Blanco, 8 février 1873 (FR).

14. B. Seiller, *Droit administratif* (Flammarion 2016).
15. 2005 Belgian Space Law, Art. 11.

Article 10 Register of Authorizations*

The Minister shall keep a public register of authorizations granted under this law, according to the terms established by the Grand-Ducal regulation.

I. DRAFTING HISTORY

Article 10 of the 2020 Law on Space Activities already appeared in the original Draft of the Law.[1] Its inclusion serves the purpose of informing the public about authorizations of space activities granted by Luxembourg. Both the Chamber of Commerce and the Conseil d'État had no comments on the Article, whose text has remained exactly the same throughout the drafting process of the Law.

II. INTERPRETATION

Article 10 of the 2020 Law on Space Activities establishes a public register listing the authorizations of space activities granted by the authorities of Luxembourg. As mentioned in the explanatory note attached to the original project of the Law, the purpose of this Article is to inform the public about planned and ongoing space activities.[2] Within the domestic framework of Luxembourg, the provision serves the purpose of guaranteeing the accountability of space missions. Naturally, the actual impact of this provision will depend on the amount of information that will be included in the Register, based upon the relevant implementing regulation. To protect sensitive information of commercial or security nature, it is likely that the public register will contain mostly general information on the authorization holder, the nature, location, and time of operations, as well as a summary of the main authorization conditions.
Within international space law, this provision could be connected to Article XI of the OST, which establishes a mechanism to share information on space activities with the

* Antonino Salmeri
1. 2018 Law on Draft Space Activities, p. 4.
2. *Id.* at p. 15.

goal "to promote international cooperation in the peaceful exploration and use of outer space."[3] According to this provision, "States agree to inform the Secretary General of the United Nations, as well as the public and the international scientific community, to the greatest extent feasible and practical, of the nature, conduct, locations and results of such activities."[4] While the Luxembourgish legislator did not make any direct reference to Article XI OST, it would be certainly desirable that the information included in the public Register established under Article 10 of the 2020 Law would also be transmitted to the UN Secretary General in accordance with Article XI OST, so that the latter can "disseminate it immediately and effectively."[5]

It is important to keep in mind that the text of the earlier 2017 Law on Space Resources does not include a similar provision and the 2020 Law on Space Activities of Luxembourg generally does not apply to space resource activities. From a systemic viewpoint, this creates an important discrepancy within the national space legislation of Luxembourg that will hopefully be addressed in the near future by the Luxembourgish legislator.

Finally, it should be noted that the scope of Article 10 of the 2020 Law on Space Activities is different than the one of Article 15 within the same Law setting up a National Register of Space Objects. This is because the former deals with the domestic authorizations of space activities, while the latter concerns the national and international registration of space objects. Accordingly, the inclusion of an authorized space activity in the Register established under Article 10 of the 2020 Law on Space Activities does not have any direct impact on the status of Luxembourg as State of Registry for any of the space objects involved.

III. EVALUATION

Article 10 of the 2020 Law on Space Activities is one of the few provisions in the global realm of national space legislations that establishes a public register listing granted authorizations for space activities. While many countries have established national registers for space objects, only few of them have done it also for space activities in general. Among those, Article 14(3) of the 2005 Belgian Space Law obliges the competent Minister to keep an up-to-date and public register of authorizations issued pursuant to the Law, including the terms and conditions attached to each authorization.[6] In the US, this responsibility is directly tackled by federal agencies. The Federal Aviation Authority maintains an online database of licensed launches,[7] and the Federal Communications Commission has one for frequency assignments.[8]

3. Outer Space Treaty, Art. XI.
4. *Id.*
5. *Id.*
6. 2005 Belgian Space Law, Art. 11, paras. 4-5.
7. Federal Aviation Administration, Licensed Launches, https://www.faa.gov/data_research/commercial_space_data/launches/ (accessed April 2022).
8. Federal Communications Commission, FCC Frequency Assignment Databases, https://www.fcc.gov/fcc-frequency-assignment-databases (accessed April 2022).

Article 11 Supervision*

Operators authorized to carry out space activity under Article 5 shall be subject to the Minister's continuous supervision.

I. DRAFTING HISTORY

Article 11 appeared in the original Draft of the 2020 Law with a much longer text,[1] which has been almost entirely deleted throughout the drafting process. Originally, the provision included seven paragraphs partially addressing the extent and scope of the Minister's power to supervise.

Former paragraph 2 established that the Minister exercises its attributions exclusively in the public interest, and that the State cannot be held responsible or liable for the fault of the operator or others.[2] In its Opinion of November 11, 2018,[3] the Chamber of Commerce criticized the complete exoneration of liability for the State as contrary to the jurisprudence of the Constitutional Court, in light of the lack of proportionality.[4] In its Opinion of February 15, 2019,[5] the Conseil d'État upheld these concerns and formally opposed the part of this paragraph providing for the State exoneration of responsibility and liability.[6] According to the Conseil, this exoneration would be a violation of Articles VI and VII of the OST, under which States are respectively responsible for their national activities in space and liable for damages caused by their launched space objects.[7] On July 20, 2020, the Commission of Economy implemented the decision of the Conseil by removing this paragraph from Article 11.[8]

* Antonino Salmeri
1. 2018 Draft Law on Space Activities, p. 5.
2. *Id.*
3. Avis de la Chambre de Commerce (November 19, 2018).
4. *Id.* at 12.
5. Avis du Conseil d'État (February 15, 2019).
6. *Id.* at 7-8.
7. Outer Space Treaty, Arts. VI-VII OST.
8. Avis de la Chambre de Commerce (November 19, 2018) 12.

Former paragraphs 3-7 partially addressed the powers attributed to the Minister in the exercise of its supervision attributions.[9] It is important to note that these paragraphs were originally included also in the 2017 Law on Space Resources and had been removed pursuant to the Opinion of the Conseil of April 7, 2017.[10] First, the Minister had the power to be assisted by external experts. Second, at any moment, the operator was obliged to provide all necessary access for inspection and verification purposes. Third, within these processes, the external experts were given access to all the necessary information and data located in any place directly or indirectly connected with the space activity. Complementarily, paragraph 5 further provided the power to access even domiciles, although with some limitations concerning certain time intervals. Pursuant to paragraph 6, in the course of these inspections and visits, the involved administrative personnel and experts were subject to professional secrecy under Article 458 of the Luxembourg Criminal Code[11] and had to possess the necessary accreditation in case of classified documents or technologies. Finally, in case the operator would refuse access to the information or data requested, under paragraph 7 the Minister could either suspend or withdraw the authorization or sanction the operator. In its Opinion of November 11, 2018,[12] the Chamber de Commerce criticized these paragraphs on two main grounds: the lack of details concerning the supervision procedure and the absence of any requirements concerning the qualities and the competences of the external experts.[13]

In its Opinion of February 15, 2019,[14] the Conseil formally opposed paragraphs 5 and 7.[15] According to the Conseil, paragraph 5 violated Article 15 of the Luxembourg Constitution, as well as Article 8 of the European Convention on Human Rights[16] because it allowed for domicile inspections and visits without the previous authorization of a judge.[17] For what concerns paragraph 7, the Conseil referred to its observations under Article 9 of the 2020 Law on Space Activities on the lack of proportionality.[18] On July 20, 2020, the Commission of Economy decided to remove all these paragraphs to ensure coherence with the earlier 2017 Law on Space Resources, from which a similar provision had been removed, as well as to implement the comments of the Conseil.[19] As a consequence, the first paragraph of Article 11 became its only provision.

9. 2018 Draft Law on Space Activities, p. 5.
10. Avis du Conseil d'État (April 7, 2017).
11. Code du 16 juin 1879—Code Pénal.
12. Avis de la Chambre de Commerce (November 19, 2018).
13. *Id.* at 12.
14. Avis du Conseil d'État (February 15, 2019).
15. *Id.* at 8.
16. European Convention for the Protection of Human Rights and Fundamental Freedoms, as amended by Protocols Nos. 11 and 14, November 4, 1950, ETS 5.
17. *Id.*
18. *Id.* at 6, 8.
19. Amendements parlementaires (July 20, 2020) 12.

II. INTERPRETATION

Article 11 of the 2020 Law on Space Activities places authorized operators under the continuous supervision of the competent Minister for space. As mentioned earlier, this provision complements Article 3 of the 2020 Law on Space Activities, according to which operators shall conduct their space activities respecting the conditions of the authorization and the international obligations of the State. To ensure compliance with this provision, the Minister is given the power to continuously supervise the operator in the conduct of the authorized space activity. Both Articles implement the international obligations stemming from Article VI of the OST, according to which nongovernmental activities in space shall require the authorization and continuing supervision of the appropriate State, which shall also assure their conformity to the OST provisions.[20] It is important to note that the duty to supervise implies an obligation of due diligence,[21] which means that States have to actively verify the legitimate conduct of private activities in outer space.[22]

Because of the amendments to the original text of the provision, it is unclear how exactly the Minister will exercise its powers/duties to supervise the authorized space activities. Based upon the two Opinions expressed by the Conseil d'État on April 7, 2017[23] and February 15, 2019,[24] it can be assumed that the Minister will have to directly supervise through its institutional structure, and that any visit and inspection will have to be conducted in accordance with applicable constitutional requirements. Having said that, further details on supervision can be expected within the relevant implementing regulations. Finally, it should be noted that under Article 8(1) of the 2020 Law on Space Activities the Minister may add specific provisions addressing the supervision procedure for a given space activity within its authorization document. This allows for further flexibility in adapting the supervising process to the features and needs of the various activities authorized.

III. EVALUATION

The comparative evaluation of Article 11 of the Law on Space Activities leads to different results depending on the chosen term of comparison. If compared to the homologue provisions within the 2008 French Space Act, i.e., Articles 7 and 8,[25] the Luxembourgish rule is rather short and general. These two Articles of the French law in fact provide for a detailed distribution among various administrative entities of strong supervision powers, including to request and copy documents as well as to visit and inspect buildings and facilities (including residencies, but only with the previous

20. Outer Space Treaty, Art. VI.
21. Bin Cheng, *Studies in International Space Law* (2004) 188. Antonio Cassese, *International Law* (2005) 168.
22. Tanja Masson-Zwaan, "Article VI of the Outer Space Treaty and Private Human Access to Space," in *Proceedings of the 51st Colloquium on the Law of Outer Space* (2009) 537.
23. Avis du Conseil d'État (April 7, 2017).
24. Avis du Conseil d'État (February 15, 2019).
25. 2008 French Space Act, Arts. 7-8.

authorization of a judge).[26] Considering that the Conseil d'État only opposed two of the seven initial paragraphs of Article 11 of the Draft,[27] it may be argued that the Luxembourgish legislator had been perhaps too "drastic" in essentially removing all substantive content from the provision. On the other hand, there are also examples of space legislations not directly providing a specific procedure for supervision. For instance, Article 6 of the 2005 Belgian Space Law delegates the decision on the conditions for the supervision of space activities to further implementing regulation.[28] In this respect, it is desirable that the Luxembourgish regulator enacts these regulations as early as possible, to provide operators with the legal certainty needed to conduct their activities.

26. *Id.*
27. Avis du Conseil d'État (February 15, 2019) 7-8.
28. 2005 Belgian Space Law, Art. 6.

Article 12 Transfer*

(1) Unless authorized by the Minister in advance, any transfer to a third party of the space activities authorized or of real or personal rights, including guarantee rights, involving the transfer of actual control over the space object, shall be prohibited.

For the purposes of this article, "actual control" shall be deemed to mean: the authority exercised over the activation of the means of control or telecommand and, where appropriate, the associated monitoring devices, required for the execution of the launch, flight operation or guidance activities of one or more space objects.

(2) Requests for authorization to transfer shall be made jointly by the transferor operator and the transferee operator.

(3) All the provisions applicable to the authorization referred to in Article 6, paragraph 1, sections 2 et seq. and in paragraphs 2 to 4 shall apply to the authorization to transfer.

(4) When the transferee operator is not established in the Grand Duchy of Luxembourg, the Minister shall refuse transfer authorization in the absence of a special agreement with the State of which the transferee operator is a national or which has international liability for the space activities thereof and which guarantees the Luxembourg State against any recourse brought against it on account of its international liability or for compensation for loss or damage.

I. DRAFTING HISTORY

In contrast to the 2017 Law on Space Resources, the authors of the 2020 Law on Space Activities included in the text of the document a specific provision regulating the

* Laetitia Zarkan and P.J. Blount

procedure of a transfer of authorized space activity. Its inspiration was the Recommendation No. 8 of the UN Resolution 68/74 on national legislation relevant to the peaceful exploration and use of outer space (Recommendation No. 8).[1] Its substance has not changed during the legislative procedure, but several details have changed.

Pursuant to Article 5(5) of the 2020 Law, the authorization given for space activities is personal and nontransferable. Therefore, the 2018 Draft Law subjected any request for transfer of the authorized activities to a third party to an application for authorization.[2]

Concerning the terms used in the provision, the Conseil d'État having approved the use of the terms *cession d'activités spatiales* and *droits de garantie*, which also appear in the 2005 Belgian Space Law,[3] it formally requested for a definition of "effective control" used in the 2018 Draft, to prevent any legal uncertainty.[4] At the session of the Commission of Economy, the representatives of the Ministry welcomed the proposition of the Conseil d'État requiring this definition and added subparagraph to paragraph 1, clarifying what is meant by effective control of a space object.[5] The proposed definition has been modeled on that provided by the Belgian legislator in Article 3, paragraph 3, of the 2005 Belgian Space Law.

Paragraph 2 of the Article in its form of 2018 stated that the application for authorization to transfer must be made by the transferee operator. However, in order to avoid applications for transfer authorization of which the transferor is unaware, the Conseil d'État recommended that the application for transfer authorization must also come from the transferor.[6] If the transferee has to disclose to the competent Minister confidential information which the transferee does not want to reveal to the transferor, the transferor and the transferee may submit separate applications, as is the case under the 1993 Law on the Financial Sector. The parliamentary Commission of Economy accommodated the suggestion of the Conseil d'État that the request for transfer should also come from the transferor in order to avoid requests of which the transferor is not aware.[7]

Paragraphs 4 and 5 of the 2018 Draft formulated the conditions for the authorization of a transfer, including the right given to the Minister to attach "additional conditions to the transfer authorization which are binding on either the transferee operator or the transferring operator or both." The Conseil d'État considered that the

1. UNGA Resolution 68/74, Recommendation No. 8.
2. 2018 Draft Law on Space Activities, Commentaire des articles, p. 8.
3. 2005 Belgian Space Law, Art. 13.
4. Avis du Conseil d'État (February 15, 2019) 8.
5. Amendements parlementaires (July 20, 2020) 13.
6. Avis du Conseil d'État (February 15, 2019) 8.
7. Rapport de la Commission de l'Economie, de la Protection des Consommateurs et de l'Espace (December 2, 2020). 15.

right to impose undefined additional conditions violated Article 11(6) of the Constitution of Luxembourg as a restriction on the freedom of trade.[8] Therefore, the Commission of Economy decided to delete paragraph 4 which allowed the Minister to "attach additional conditions to the transfer authorization."[9]

In the event that the transferee is not established in Luxembourg, the authors of the Draft considered that the authorization may be refused as long as Luxembourg does not obtain the necessary guarantees from the State of which the transferee is a national or to which the space activities would belong after the transfer, in order to be covered by that State in the event of the liability of Luxembourg being called into play. Therefore, the decision may be subject to specific conditions to be met by the transferor and/or the transferee.[10] Such a principle is based on the fact that Luxembourg is a launching State of a space object and therefore retains liability even after its transfer to an operator belonging to another State.[11] On this point, the Chamber of Commerce approved the conditions set out in the Draft but criticized the fact that the provisions relating to the transfer of activity do not mention the case of the arrival in Luxembourg of operators whose activities are already the subject of authorizations in due form abroad.[12] About the notion of a "third party" within the meaning of the original paragraph 5, the Conseil d'État noted that this reference was linked to the transferee operator and must be designated as such.[13] This recommendation was reflected in the final Draft of Article 12.[14]

The central condition of authorization of transfer of an authorized space activity is an existence of a bilateral agreement between Luxembourg and the State of the transferee. On this condition, the Conseil d'État considered that the transfer of space activities is subject to a situation that is not within the control of the transferee and that will not be fulfilled quickly. For the Conseil d'État, the international agreement will still have to be approved and ratified by the national authorities in accordance with the constitutional orders of the States—Parties to the agreement. Therefore, the Conseil d'État asked how the transferee or the transferor could possibly challenge the absence of such an agreement between States before the Luxembourg administrative courts, assuming that the conclusion of treaties constitutes a sovereign power of a State which is not justiciable before a national judicial or administrative jurisdiction.[15]

Furthermore, the use of the phrase "the Minister may refuse authorization" in the original version of this paragraph lead to the conclusion that authorization for a transfer of space activities may be granted even in the absence of bilateral agreement required by the provision. The Conseil d'État saw in the power to refuse or authorize the transfer of space activities, in the absence of precise criteria laid down by law, a

8. Avis du Conseil d'État (February 15, 2019) 9 and Constitution coordonnée du Grand-Duché de Luxembourg, Mémorial A N° 23, 22 octobre 1868, Art. 11.
9. Amendements parlementaires (July 20, 2020) 13.
10. 2018 Draft Law on Space Activities, p. 16.
11. *Id.*
12. Avis de la Chambre de Commerce (November 19, 2018) 13.
13. 2018 Law on Draft Space Activities, 9.
14. Amendements parlementaires (July 20, 2020).
15. 2018 Draft Law on Space Activities, p. 9.

violation of Article 11(6) of the Constitution,[16] and formally objected to the paragraph 5 as initially drafted, while noting that the text is also contained in the 2005 Belgian Space Law.[17] The Commission of Economy turned the possibility of refusing authorization for the transfer of space activities in the absence of such agreement into an obligation, and the text was rephrased into the clear "the Minister shall refuse authorization."[18]

II. INTERPRETATION

Article 12 is first mentioned at the fifth paragraph of Article 5 as the exception to the personal and nonassignable nature of the authorization. It sets out the process for an operator to transfer space activities to another operator. As a general rule, such transfer is prohibited without explicit permission from the authorizing Minister. Specifically, this applies to any transfer that affects the "actual control" of the space object, which represents the authority over the means of control or telecommand of a space activity.

To gain permission for such a transfer, the transferor and the transferee must present a joint application to the authorizing Minister that shows that the transferee meets specific provisions in Article 6, paragraph 1, sections 2 et seq. and paragraphs 2-4. If the transferee is a non-Luxembourgish entity, then the transfer will not be able to occur unless there is a bilateral agreement with either the State of nationality of the transferee or a State that has international liability for the space activities of the transferee. This bilateral agreement must guarantee to indemnify Luxembourg for any liability resulting from the space activity of the transferee.

III. EVALUATION

Article 12 is based on Article 13, paragraph 1, of the 2005 Belgian Space Law, as it provides a definition of the notion of "effective control."[19] The Belgian law defines this term as "the authority exercised over the activation of the means of command or remote control and, where appropriate, of the associated means of surveillance, necessary for the execution of the activities of launching, flight operation or guidance of one or more space objects."

The 2008 French Space Act includes additional provisions on transfer of space activities in the part dealing with authorization.[20] The provisions of the Act put such transfer of activities at the same level as launching or operating a space object and therefore, the new operator has to comply with the same rules as if the activity or the object had never been authorized. This allows the authorities to make sure the new operator will comply with equivalent obligations.

---

16. Constitution coordonnée du Grand-Duché de Luxembourg, Mémorial A N° 23, 22 octobre 1868, Art. 11.
17. 2018 Draft Law on Space Activities, p. 9, and 2005 Belgian Space Law.
18. Amendements parlementaires (July 20, 2020).
19. 2005 Belgian Space Law, Art. 13.
20. 2008 French Space Act, Art. 3.

Article 13 Change of Control*

(1) Any natural or legal person that has taken the decision to acquire or increase, either directly or indirectly, a qualifying holding in an operator, resulting in the proportion of capital units or voting rights held amounting to or exceeding the thresholds of 20%, 30% or 50% or such operator becoming its subsidiary, shall inform the Minister of its intention in advance in writing.

(2) Any natural or legal person that has taken the decision to transfer, either directly or indirectly, a qualifying holding or to reduce its qualifying holding so that the proportion of capital units or voting rights held amounts to less than the thresholds of 20%, 30% or 50% or the operator ceases to be its subsidiary, shall inform the Minister of its intention in advance in writing.

(3) The potential acquirer of a qualifying holding shall provide the Minister with information indicating the amount of the holding envisaged. The Minister shall publish a list specifying the information required to assess the notification having to be submitted to him at the time of notification.

(4) If the influence exercised by a potential acquirer referred to in paragraph 3 is likely to be exercised to the detriment of sound and prudent operation by the operator, the Minister shall object thereto or take appropriate measures to end such a situation.

For the purposes of section 1, the Minister may suspend exercise of the voting rights attached to the shares or units held by the shareholders or partners concerned.

When a holding is acquired despite the Minister's objection, the Minister may suspend exercise of the corresponding voting rights or request the nullity or invalidation of the votes cast.

The Minister may take the same measures in respect of natural or legal persons that fail to observe the obligation to provide prior information provided for by this article.

---

* Laetitia Zarkan and P.J. Blount

The measures provided for in this paragraph may be the subject of an appeal for reversal before the administrative court ruling on the substance of the case.

(5) Every operator shall be required to inform the Minister, as soon as it becomes aware thereof, of any acquisitions or transfers of qualifying holdings in its capital.

I. DRAFTING HISTORY

Article 13 in its form of the 2018 Draft Law on Space Activities was formulated in a way that any person who would acquire or dispose of a qualifying interest in the operator that has a license for a space activity would be required to notify the operator without delay. In this case, the operator who becomes aware of such a plan shall likewise immediately inform the Minister. When a person would have exceeded the threshold of 20% of the voting rights, the Minister could even withdraw or suspend the authorization granted to an operator if this person coming to hold directly or indirectly such a participation does not offer all the moral, financial, professional and technical guarantees provided for in Article 6 of the Law.[1]

This Article has undergone several changes during the legislative process. First, as underlined by the Chamber of Commerce, Article 13 set out the obligation to notify immediately and "without delay," from the legal person to the operator and then from the operator to the Minister, upon the acquisition or disposal of a qualifying interest in the operator. The Chamber proposed to the authors of the 2018 Draft to define the term "without delay" and to specify the time limits directly in the provision of the Article,[2] a position which has been supported by the Conseil d'État.[3]

Second, the Conseil d'État qualified paragraph 1 of Article 13 as "confusing," considering that it provided that a person "acquiring or disposing" of a qualifying holding must notify the operator without delay and that the operator must notify the Minister as soon as he becomes aware of such a "plan."[4] The Conseil d'État underlined that the first sentence of this paragraph referred to an acquisition or disposal, i.e., a transaction that would have already taken place, whereas the last sentence refers to a specific "plan."[5] The Conseil reminded that Article 6(5) of the 1993 Law on the Financial Sector, which served as an model for this provision, refers to a person who "has taken the decision to acquire, directly or indirectly, a qualifying holding in a credit institution," not mentioning any further "plan." It also underlined that the same wording was used in Article 87 of the 2015 Law on the Insurance Sector.[6]

1. 2018 Draft Law on Space Activities, Commentaire des articles, p. 16.
2. Avis de la Chambre de Commerce (November 19, 2018) 13.
3. Avis du Conseil d'État (February 15, 2019) 9.
4. *Id.*
5. *Id.*
6. Law of December 7, 2015 on the Insurance Sector, Mémorial A N° 229 (December 9, 2015), Art. 87:

On the notion of "qualifying holding," it has been defined in the Draft at Article 2(5) as the direct or indirect holding in an undertaking of 10% or more of the capital or of the voting rights or any other possibility of exercising a significant influence on the management of that undertaking.[7] This definition is based on Article 1(25) of the 1993 Law on the Financial Sector, setting the threshold at 10% of the capital or voting rights.[8] For the determination of the level of participation, the Commentary of the 2018 Draft Law on Space Activities[9] refers also to Articles 8, 9 and 10 of the 2008 Law on Transparency Requirements for Issuers of Securities,[10] which transposes Directive 2004/109/EC of the European Parliament and of the Council of December 15, 2004 on Transparency Requirements for Issuers whose Securities are Admitted to Trading on a Regulated Market.

As noted in the 2019 Opinion of the Conseil d'État, the 2018 Draft did not include the obligation to require prior authorization from the competent Minister before the transfer or acquisition of a qualifying holding. On this point, the Conseil d'État reminded that the laws governing the financial and insurance sectors provide for a request for prior authorization by the Minister to be made by the proposed acquirer, the transferor and the company concerned. The Conseil d'État underlined the fact that the trigger would not be the transfer or acquisition of a qualifying holding, but the crossing of the 10% or 20% threshold. Therefore, the Conseil suggested to reword the paragraph in the sense that the notification obligation arises when a person intends to acquire a holding so that the proportion of voting rights or capital held by him reaches or exceeds the 10% or 20% thresholds, or when a shareholder intends to dispose of his holding so that the proportion of voting rights or capital held by him falls below the 10% or 20% thresholds.[11]

Acquisitions: Any natural or legal person, whether acting alone or in concert with other persons ("the proposed acquirer") who have taken a decision either to acquire, directly or indirectly, a qualifying holding in a Luxembourg insurance or reinsurance undertaking or to further increase, directly or indirectly, such a qualifying holding in a Luxembourg insurance or reinsurance undertaking as a result of which the proportion of the voting rights or of the capital held would reach or exceed 20 %, 30 % or 50 % or so that the insurance or reinsurance undertaking would become its subsidiary ("the proposed acquisition"), shall first notify in writing the CAA of their intention to acquire or increase a qualifying holding, indicating the size of the intended holding and relevant information, as referred to in Article 89, paragraph 3. Any natural or legal person who has taken a decision to dispose, directly or indirectly, of a qualifying holding in a Luxembourg insurance or reinsurance undertaking shall first notify in writing the CAA of its intention, indicating the size of that person's holding after the intended disposal. Such natural or legal person shall likewise notify the CAA in advance of a decision to reduce that person's qualifying holding so that the proportion of the voting rights or of the capital held would fall below 20 %, 30 % or 50 % or so that the insurance or reinsurance undertaking would cease to be a subsidiary of that person.

7. 2018 Draft Law on Space Activities, Art. 2.
8. 1993 Law on the Financial Sector, Article 1.
9. 2018 Draft Law on Space Activities, p. 9.
10. Law of January 11, 2008 on Transparency Requirements for Issuers of Securities, Mémorial A N° 5, 2008, Arts. 8-10.
11. Avis du Conseil d'État (February 15, 2019) 9.

To comply with the request of the Conseil d'État, the Commission of Economy reworded paragraph 1 of Article 13(1), while relying on paragraphs 4-7 of Article 12 of the 2009 Law on Payment Services[12] for the following provisions of Article 13 in its new wording to keep consistency.[13] Interestingly, the Conseil d'État noted that such a provision does not appear in the 2017 Law on Space Resources, despite the desire of the authors of the amendments to ensure consistency between it and the 2020 Law on Space Activities.[14]

The original paragraph 2 provided for suspension or withdrawal of authorization as consequences of the fact that a person who exceeded 20% voting rights does not fulfill the guarantees formulated in Article 6 of the 2020 Law. With this regard, the Conseil d'État recommended to move this provision to Article 8 of the 2020 Law on Space Activities as one of the conditions for issuing an authorization. The rules on suspension or withdrawal of the authorization would thus take place in accordance with Article 9.[15]

In the debates of the parliamentary Commission on Economy, the representatives of the Ministry pointed out that the Minister had a duty to ensure that "sound and prudent management" of the operators would be guaranteed; therefore, in the new version of Article 13, in case that the influence exercised by a potential acquirer of a qualified holding is likely to be exercised to its detriment, the Minister was given the right to take appropriate measures to end such situation.[16] The Minister's reaction would depend on the concrete situation encountered and may range from the suspension of the exercise of the respective voting rights to the withdrawal of the authorization granted, pursuant to Article 9 of the 2018 Draft Law on Space Activities.[17] In paragraph 4, subparagraph 1, the Conseil d'État asked the authors of the Draft to replace the notion of "sound and prudent management" with "sound and prudent

12. Law on Payment Services of November 10, 2009, Mémorial A N° 215, 2009, Art. 12(4):

> Any natural or legal person who has taken a decision to acquire or to further increase, directly or indirectly, a qualifying holding within the meaning of point (34) of Article 1 in a payment institution, as a result of which the proportion of the capital or of the voting rights held would reach or exceed 20 per cent, 30 per cent or 50 per cent, or so that the payment institution would become its subsidiary, shall inform the CSSF in writing of its intention in advance. Any natural or legal person who has taken a decision to dispose, directly or indirectly, of a qualifying holding, or to reduce its qualifying holding so that the proportion of the capital or of the voting rights held would fall below 20 per cent, 30 per cent or 50 per cent, or so that the payment institution would cease to be its subsidiary, shall inform the CSSF in writing of its intention in advance. The proposed acquirer of a qualifying holding shall supply to the CSSF information indicating the size of the intended holding. The CSSF shall make publicly available a list specifying the information that is necessary to carry out the assessment of the notification and that must be provided to it at the time of notification.

13. Amendements parlementaires (July 20, 2020) 15.
14. Avis complémentaire du Conseil d'État (September 29, 2020) 3.
15. Avis du Conseil d'État (February 15, 2019) 10.
16. Amendements parlementaires (July 20, 2020).
17. Commission de l'Economie, de la Protection des consommateurs et de l'Espace; Commission de l'Environnement, du Climat, de l'Energie et de l'Aménagement du territoire, Procès-verbal de la réunion du 18 juin 2020, p. 4.

operation" already used in Article 6 of the Draft law. The Conseil d'État justified this request by stating that using two different terms in the same law may lead to discussions on their differences.[18] Taking into account the opinion of the Conseil d'État, the Commission of Economy decided to make this replacement.[19]

As a result, considering the Opinion of the Conseil d'État, the Commission of Economy completely reformulated Article 13.[20] With regard to this new version that encompassed the right of the operator to bring an action against the measures taken by the Minister before the administrative court in the one-month time limit,[21] the Conseil d'État proposed that the one-month time limit to be deleted from the text. It considered that, since the one-month time limit is specific to financial sector legislation, there is nothing to prevent the application of the ordinary three-month time limit to the proposed law.[22] The Commission of Economy accepted this suggestion, thus the ordinary legislation period of three months applies.[23]

II. INTERPRETATION

Pursuant to Article 13, changes in qualified holdings must be notified to the Minister in writing before these changes occur. Specifically, the Minister must be informed of changes that results "in the proportion of capital units or voting rights held amounting to or exceeding the thresholds of 20%, 30%, or 50%" or changes that affect the status of the operator as a subsidiary of another organization. This applies to both those possessing a qualified holding and those that intend to acquire a qualified holding. The Minister is required to provide a list of information needed for assessment and to be disclosed as part of this notification. If the Minister determines that this change will affect the "sound and prudent operation" of the space activity then she/he may object to the transfer. The Minister may suspend the voting rights associated with this share if the transfer occurs despite the objection or if the transfer occurs without prenotification. Any such decision is appealable through administrative court. The final section of this Article places a duty on the operator to inform the Minister of any changes in its qualified holdings.

III. EVALUATION

Article 13 is very specific to Luxembourg as its wording was initially almost identical to Article 12(4-7) of the 2009 Law on Payment Services.[24] There are no similar provisions in other space laws. This provision is indeed interesting as it touches on the notions of

18. Avis complémentaire du Conseil d'État (September 29, 2020) 3.
19. Rapport de la Commission de l'Economie, de la Protection des consommateurs et de l'Espace, Commentaire des articles (December 2, 2020) 12.
20. Amendements parlementaires (July 20, 2020) 14.
21. *Id.*
22. Avis complémentaire du Conseil d'État (September 29, 2020) 3.
23. Rapport de la Commission de l'Economie, de la Protection des consommateurs et de l'Espace, Commentaire des articles (December 2, 2020) 12.
24. Law on Payment Services of November 10, 2009, Mémorial A N° 215, 2009, Art. 12.

continuing supervision and protecting the State from liability. The ongoing "sound and prudent" operation of the space activity seems to be a paramount concern of the State, and as a result strict measures are imposed to ensure the suitability of individuals and entities that can influence the direction of an operator.

Article 14 Sanctions*

(1) Anyone who has infringed or attempted to infringe Articles 3, 5, paragraph 1, or 12, paragraph 1 or paragraph 4 shall be penalized with imprisonment from eight days to five years and a fine of 5,000 euros to 1,250,000 euros or just one of these penalties.

(2) Anyone who has infringed or attempted to infringe the provisions of Articles 5, paragraph 5, 6, paragraph 1, section 5, 6, paragraph 5, sections 1 and 2, or the terms of the authorization, respectively, shall be penalized by imprisonment from eight days to one year and a fine of 1,250 euros to 500,000 euros or just one of these penalties.

(3) Without prejudice to paragraphs 1 and 2, the court applied to may pronounce termination of the space activity contrary to the provision of this Law under a penalty of a fine whose maximum amount may not exceed 1,000,000 euros per day of infringement established.

I. DRAFTING HISTORY

Through the legislative process, Article 14 of the Law on Space Activities has undergone significant changes pursuant to the formal opposition expressed by the Conseil d'État on several points.[1] It is interesting to note, however, that the Chamber of Commerce made no comment.

The 2018 Draft Law on Space Activities initially included two provisions dealing with sanctions: Article 14 and Article 15. While the latter dealt with criminal sanctions, Draft Article 14 attempted to introduce administrative sanctions in the legal framework regulating space activities. Contrary to the 2017 Law on Space Resources,[2] the 2020 Law on Space Activities in its first draft distinguished between authorized operators

* Gabrielle Leterre
1. Avis du Conseil d'État (February 15, 2019) 10.
2. *See* 2017 Law on Space Resources, Art. 18.

and operators carrying out space activities without governmental authorization, or under an authorization obtained by false means. Thus, the authorized operators would be exposed to administrative sanctions whereas nonauthorized operators would face criminal sanctions. The administrative sanctions could take the form of a fine decided by the Minister in charge within the limit of EUR 500,000 and/or issue an official reprimand to the operator.[3]

Ultimately, the Conseil d'État formulated several oppositions on the administrative sanction regime. It first stressed the need to harmonize the sanction regime under the 2020 Law on Space Activities with the one already established under the 2017 Law on Space Resources in order to avoid discrepancies for operators operating under both the 2017 and the 2020 regimes.

Furthermore, the Conseil d'État noted *inter alia* that Draft Article 14, paragraph 1(a) called for penalties in cases where an operator violated obligations determined in the authorization document even though Draft Article 5 did not list such obligations. The Draft provision also failed to establish a timeframe during which a repeated offense could be sanctioned by doubling the amount of the original fine. The Conseil d'État also remarked that there was no graduation for the administrative penalties, nor any framework to regulate the Minister's power to make public administrative sanctions imposed to operators. In contrast, the 1993 Law on the Financial Sector,[4] which served as a basis for the 2020 Law on Space Activities, provides a detailed regime regarding the publication of administrative sanctions by the Financial Sector Supervisory Commission.[5]

Based on the strong concerns expressed by the Conseil d'État and the fact that no equivalent exists in the 2017 Law on Space Resources, the Commission of Economy decided to address these concerns by removing Draft Article 14 from the Law. It further decided to amend Draft Article 15 to reflect the content of Article 18 of the 2017 Law on Space Resources.[6] In a complementary opinion, the Conseil d'État remarked that if the intension was to align the regime for sanction with the 2017 Law on Space Resources, then it should be done completely and only violations sanctioned in the first law should be sanctioned in the new law.[7]

II. INTERPRETATION

Article 14 of the General Space Law defines the criminal sanctions for the violation, or attempt to violate, the provisions of the Law. In particular, paragraph 1 defines a term of imprisonment between eight days and five years and/or a fine of EUR 5,000 to EUR 1,250,000 for any person who carries out a space activity without having been granted

3. 2018 Draft Law on Space Activities, Art. 14.
4. 1993 Law on the Financial Sector.
5. For instance, depending on the violation, the administrative penalties imposed either must be published on the Commission website or shall only be published if appropriate and necessary. 1993 Law on the Financial Sector, Art. 63-3.
6. Rapport de la Commission de l'Economie, de la Protection des Consommateurs et de l'Espace (December 2, 2020) 15-16.
7. Avis complémentaire du Conseil d'État (September 29, 2020) 4.

a mission authorization by the Minister in charge prior to the beginning of the activity; does not comply with the conditions of the mission authorization and Luxembourg's international obligations, such as *inter alia* the ones defined in the ratified UN Space Treaties;[8] or transfers to a third party the "effective control" of a space object by transferring to them authorized space activities or real or personal rights, without prior authorization from the Minister.[9]

Paragraph 2 defines a different set of sanctions for any person who contravenes, or attempts to contravene, the following obligations. First, as the mission authorization is personal and cannot be handed over to a third party, except in the cases provided for under Article 12 of the 2020 Law on Space Activities (the transfer to a third party must be authorized by the Minister in charge). Second, the management body of the operator must be constituted of at least two persons who, through their professional experience, have objectively gained the capacity to determine the direction of space activity effectively. Third, the activity carried out must comply with the terms of the mission authorization. Finally, the account must be audited every year by one or more adequate auditors. Also, any change of in the person of these auditors must be authorized by the Minister in charge. The failure for anyone to adhere to these obligations is punished by a term of imprisonment from eight days to one year and/ or a fine of EUR 1,250 to EUR 500,000.

Additionally, under paragraph 3, the authority in charge may request the courts to decide the establishment of a penalty that may not exceed EUR 1,000,000 per day of infringement until the activity which is violating the Law be ceased. Surprisingly, the provision is taken from the amended 2002 Law on the Protection of Individuals Regarding the Processing of Personal Data.[10]

III. EVALUATION

Article 14 of the 2020 Law on Space Activities copies Article 18 of the 2017 Law on Space Resources. The harmonization of the 2020 Law with the 2017 Law on Space Resources offers better legal certainty to space operators in Luxembourg by ensuring those who are granted authorizations under both laws are not subjected to two

8. As of January 2021, Luxembourg is a Signing Party to three of the five UN Space Treaties: the Treaty on Principles Governing the Activities of States in the Exploration and Use of Outer Space, Including the Moon and Other Celestial Bodies, entered into force on October 10, 1967, 610 U.N.T.S. 205 (Outer Space Treaty); the Convention on International Liability for Damage Caused by Space Objects, entered into force on October 9, 1973, 961 U.N.T.S. 187 (Liability Convention); and the Convention on Registration of Objects Launched into Outer Space, entered into force September 15, 1976, 1023 U.N.T.S. 15 (Registration Convention). Luxembourg is also working on becoming a Party to the Agreement on the Rescue of Astronauts, the Return of Astronauts, and the Return of Objects Launched into Outer Space, entered into force on December 3, 1968, 672 U.N.T.S. 119 (Return and Rescue Agreement).
9. Furthermore, the Minister cannot authorize the transfer to a third party if the transferee operator is: (1) not established in Luxembourg and (2) is not under the jurisdiction of State with which Luxembourg has an agreement protecting it against recourses brought against it on account of its international liability or for compensation for loss or damage.
10. Loi du 2 août 2002 relative à la protection des personnes à l'égard du traitement des données à caractère personnel, Mémorial A N° 91, August 13, 2002.

different regimes. Furthermore, as noted in the Commentary on Article 18 of the 2017 Law on Space Resources, it is not uncommon for States to define specific sanctions for noncompliance with the legislations and conditions regulating space activities. There is no uniformity in practice with regard to the degree of sanctions. Some prescribe for financial penalties whereas other prescribe for imprisonment or both.[11] Similarly, some States label their sanctions as being administrative or criminal in nature, whereas other do not prescribe for their character.[12]

Compared to other existing sanction regimes, Luxembourg's is not insignificant. With penalties respectively capped at EUR 1,250,000[13] and EUR 500,000[14] and the possibility to accompany these fine with imprisonment, Luxembourg's leans toward the higher end of comparable sanction regime. As a mean of comparison, Belgium prescribes a fine that may not exceed EUR 25,000 and France's is limited to EUR 200,000.[15] The Dutch regime, however, is closer to Luxembourg's with an administrative penalty of up to EUR 450,000 or "10 per cent of the relevant annual sales of the company in the Netherlands, whichever is the greater."[16]

The fact that Luxembourg chose to have high penalty fines may seem harsh, but it may prove to be an effective tool in deterring operators from deviating from the Law and circumventing the authorization process.

11. For example, 1993 South African Space Act, Art. 23. *See also* 2008 French Space Act, Art. 10-11; 2005 Belgian Space Law, Art. 19. For an extended comparison with other national legislations, *see* the commentary in this volume on Art. 18 of the 2017 Law on Space Resources.
12. Ordinance of the Supreme Soviet of Ukraine, on Space Activity Law of Ukraine of November 15, 1996, No. 503/96-BP (1996) (UA), Art. 29.
13. 2020 Law on Space Activities, Art. 14, para. 1.
14. *Id.* at Art. 14, para. 2.
15. 2008 French Space Act, Arts. 10-11; 2005 Belgian Space Law, Art. 19. For an extended comparison with other national legislations, *see* the commentary in this volume on Art. 18 of the 2017 Law on Space Resources.
16. 2006 Netherlands Space Activities Law, s. 15.

Article 15 Register of Space Objects*

(1) A National Register of Space Objects, hereinafter referred to as the "Register" is set up by the Minister in charge of Space Policy and Legislation. The space objects for which the Grand Duchy of Luxembourg shall assume a registration obligation under Article VIII of the Space Treaty and Article II of the Convention on Registration of Objects Launched into Outer Space, adopted by the United Nations General Assembly in New York on 12 November 1974, shall be entered in the Register. This Register shall be public.

(2) An operator taking the initiative to launch or to procure the launch of a space object into outer space must provide the Minister with all information allowing to identify the space object, its launch, and the position it has to occupy in outer space, including the nodal period, inclination, apogee, perigee and in particular the launching date and territory or place, the main parameters of the orbit and the general function of the space object.

(3) The operator must inform the Minister without delay of any change or risk of change in the parameters of the space object, particularly the danger of unintentional de-orbiting.

(4) If the space object is marked by a registration indication or number, the operator shall inform the Minister thereof.

I. DRAFTING HISTORY

Article 15 of the 2020 Law on Space Activities appeared already in the original Draft, where it was initially listed as Article 16.[1] This Article received no comments from the Chamber of Commerce in its Opinion of November 19, 2018.[2] The Conseil d'État, in its Opinion of February 15, 2019,[3] suggested correcting the citation of the Registration

* Antonino Salmeri

1. 2018 Draft Law on Space Activities, pp. 6-7.
2. Avis de la Chambre du Commerce (November 19, 2018) 13.
3. Avis du Conseil d'État (February 15, 2019).

Convention and noted that the 2005 Belgian Space Law, referenced by the drafters in their commentary, makes the register public.[4] On July 20, 2020, the Commission of Economy renumbered this Article from 16 to 15 after suppressing Article 14 on administrative sanctions due to the formal opposition of the Conseil.[5] Further to that, the Commission amended the new Article to correct the citation of the Registration Convention, to clarify the competent Minister in charge of establishing the Register, to underline its public nature, and to expand its scope to include also procured launches.[6] Besides these changes, the text of the provision remained unaltered throughout the drafting process.

II. INTERPRETATION

Pursuant to Article 15 of the Law on Space Activities, Luxembourg established a National Register for its space objects. The impact of this provision can be assessed at three levels: legal, political and practical. Legally, Article 15 enables Luxembourg to retain jurisdiction and control over the space objects included in its register,[7] while also making it internationally liable for any damages they cause.[8] Politically, this Article signifies that Luxembourg is ready to assume the powers and responsibilities of a launching State for the space objects launched by its operators, provided that the conditions of Articles I (c) and II of the Registration Convention are met.[9] However, based on those criteria, the probability that Luxembourg will practically qualify as a launching State is rather low. Since Luxembourg does not have any spaceport nor is planning to build any, no space object can be launched from either its territory or facilities (although the possibility to launch from airplane or ship was considered during the drafting phase).[10] This means that only the governmental space objects launched by the Grand Duchy of Luxembourg or whose launch has been procured by it[11] will be entered in the Registry. The Luxembourg's Registry of space objects includes only objects launched after the entrance into force of the 2021 Registration Law.[12]

The evaluation of Article 15 is rather different from the perspective of Luxembourgish operators. This is because the mechanism laid down in Article 15 obliges them to always inform the Minister in charge of space activities of any space object they are launching or of which they are procuring the launch. Notably, the kind of

4. *Id.* at 11.
5. Amendements parlementaires (July 20, 2020) 15-16.
6. *Id.* at 16.
7. Outer Space Treaty, Art. VIII.
8. *Id.*, Art. VII.
9. 2018 Draft Law on Space Activities, p. 17.
10. Those being two of the four alternative criteria qualifying a launching State under Registration Convention, Art. I.
11. Those being the remaining two criteria for qualifying as a launching State under Registration Convention, Art. I.
12. As stated by Luxembourg Space Agency on its website (accessed November 2021). The list of space objects launched by Luxembourg before January 1, 2021 can be found on the website of the UN Office for Outer Space Affairs and has been compiled based upon information voluntarily furnished under UNGA Resolution 1721 B (XVI).

information requested mirrors those of Registration Convention's Article IV,[13] to make sure that Luxembourg can fully comply with its obligations under the Convention.[14] However, as discussed above, not all these objects will be included in the Luxembourgish Registry—perhaps almost none of them. Pursuant to paragraph 1 of Article 15 of the 2020 Law on Space Activities, only the space objects for which the Grand Duchy of Luxembourg shall assume a registration obligation under Article VIII of the OST or Registration Convention's Article II shall be entered in the Registry.[15] As clarified in the explanatory note to the Law, this evaluation is left to the competent Minister in charge of space.[16]

After verifying the information received from the operator, the Minister will decide whether or not to include the space object in the National Register,[17] based upon the criteria set forth in Articles I (c) and II of the Registration Convention. Finally, pursuant to Article 15(3) of the 2020 Law on Space Activities operators are obliged to inform the Minister of any change in the provided registration information, especially if that implies a danger of unintentional reentry.[18] The rationale for this additional obligation is mostly related to supervision purposes, with the goal to ensure that the State can always have a real understanding of its exposition in terms of responsibility and liability.

III. EVALUATION

The establishment of a national registry for space objects is an important measure of transparency and confidence building. As recalled by the Conseil d'État in its Opinion of February 15, 2019,[19] Article 15 of the 2020 Law on Space Activities has largely been inspired by Article 14 of the 2005 Belgian Space Law.[20] Other comparable provisions are Article 12 of the 2008 French Space Act,[21] Article 61 of the 2018 UK Space Industry Act,[22] Article 16 of the 2016 Portuguese Space Law[23] and section 11 of the 2006 Netherlands Space Activities Act.[24]

Even if Luxembourg will only rarely qualify as a launching State under international space law, Article 15 is still an important provision within the 2020 Law on Space

13. Precisely nodal period, inclination, apogee, perigee, launching date and territory or place, the main parameters of the orbit and the general function of the space object.
14. 2018 Draft Law on Space Activities, p. 17.
15. 2020 Law on Space Activities, Art. 15.
16. 2018 Draft Law on Space Activities, pp. 17-18.
17. *Id.*
18. 2020 Law on Space Activities, Art. 15.
19. Avis du Conseil d'État (February 15, 2019) 11.
20. Although this latter provision is much longer, requires more information from operators and also includes a detailed registration procedure to be followed by the competent Minister. 2005 Belgian Space Law, Art. 14.
21. *See also* 2008 French Space Act, Art. 12.
22. 2018 UK Space Industry Act, Art. 61.
23. Decreto-Lei n.º 16/2019 de 22 de Janeiro, Diário da República, 1.ª série — N.º 15 — 22 de janeiro de 2019, Art. 16.
24. 2006 Netherlands Space Activities Law, s. 11.

Activities. This is because there is certainly value in acquiring fundamental information on space objects launched by national operators for supervision and coordination purposes. In this regard, it is useful to recall the example of the Netherlands,[25] which regularly sends to the UN Secretary General information on the space objects launched by its nationals based upon Article XI of the OST.[26] In essence, the Netherlands divided its national registry of space objects into "UN" and "national" sections. The "UN part" lists objects for which The Netherlands qualifies as launching State under international space law. Inclusion of these objects is then notified in accordance with Article II of the Registration Convention. The "national" part includes space objects launched by Dutch operators for which The Netherlands does not qualify as launching State. This information is then notified in accordance with Article XI of the OST to facilitate international coordination and cooperation.[27]

Similarly, Luxembourg may also decide to adopt a two-sections Registry and transmit the information received on space objects under a different legal basis depending on its status as launching State.

25. For a comprehensive assessment of Dutch registration practices, *see* Tanja Masson-Zwaan, "Registration of Small Satellites and the Case of The Netherlands," in Irmgard Marboe, ed., *Small Satellites, Regulatory Challenges and Chances* (2016) 174-194.
26. For a recent example, *see* UN Doc. A/AC.105/1186. Further notifications under Art. XI of the Outer Space Treaty can be found in the UN Office for Outer Space Affairs documents repository.
27. Article XI of the Outer Space Treaty.

Article 16 Taxes*

(1) Article 4 of the amended Law of 9 July 1937 on insurance tax, known as "Versicherungssteuergesetz", shall be amended as follows:

1. **The figure "82" is inserted before the words "for contracts of insurance covering ships".**
2. **A point 9 is added worded as follows:**
3. **"9. For contracts of insurance related to space objects falling within the scope of application of Article 15 of the Law of 15 December 2020 on space activity."**

(2) Article 152bis of the amended Law of 4 December 1967 on income tax is amended as follows:

1. **In section 1, the terms "paragraphs 2 and 7" shall be replaced by the terms "sections 2 and 7".**
2. **A section 1a is inserted, worded as follows:**

"The condition indicated in section 1 shall not apply to space objects as defined in Article 2, point 4, of the Law of 15 December 2020 on space activity".

I. DRAFTING HISTORY

The text of this Article was originally numbered Article 18 and appeared for the first time in the 2018 Draft Law on Space Activities presented by the Minister of Communication and Media. It underwent only minor modifications during the revision process. It deals with two categories of tax in Luxembourg: the tax on insurance and the income tax.

As long as there was no registry of space objects in Luxembourg, space objects under the jurisdiction of Luxembourg were not subject to any tax on insurance. The inclusion of the present Article 15 which introduced a National Register of Space

* Mahulena Hofmann

Objects changed this situation. Without any further legal steps, the tax on insurance would have become applicable on space objects. This would be an unintended negative effect of the new Law as it was known that the price of insurance of space objects can be high, which is a consequence of the risks connected to launch activities, as well as the fact that (at the time of drafting of the Law) repairing or servicing space objects while in outer space was hardly possible.[1]

Furthermore, without any additional legal steps, the operators of space objects registered in Luxembourg would be unable to apply for a benefit from the income tax. Until the modifications carried out by the 2020 Law, the condition for the eligibility to apply for such benefit was the fact that the investment is physically carried out in the territory of Luxembourg or the countries of the European Economic Area.

II. INTERPRETATION

Article 16 of the 2020 Law on Space Activities remedied these effects by enlarging two tax legislations of Luxembourg.

The first one is the 1937 Law on Insurance Tax.[2] Its object is the insurance contracts for which Luxembourg is the location of the covered risk or commitment. The exemptions from this tax are enumerated in its Article 4. They include *inter alia* insurance contracts covering sea vessels registered in Luxembourg and used for navigation on the high seas (all liability arising of the use of and all damage to and loss of such vessels). Article 18 paragraph 1 of the 2020 Law on Space Activities enlarged Article 4 by a new paragraph. It added the contract of insurance related to space objects registered in Luxembourg to the exemptions from the insurance tax.

The second paragraph of Article 16 deals with the eligibility for benefits connected with the income tax. Article 152*bis* of the amended 1967 Law on Income Tax[3] allows the taxpayers to apply for tax rebates for investments made in their business. The condition for the benefit is that the business is permanently located in Luxembourg. Furthermore, the taxpayer must physically make these investments within the European Economic Area including Iceland, Liechtenstein, and Norway. To make space objects eligible for this beneficial category, the 2020 Law enlarged Article 152*bis* on income tax by a provision stating that space objects are exempted from the condition that the investment must be physically made in the European Economic Area including the three enumerated States.

Interestingly, this Article is one of the two provisions of the 2020 Law on Space Activities that are applicable also on the missions on space resources. A similar provision does not exist in the 2017 Law on Space Resources. However, Article 1 of the 2020 Law states that "this law shall not apply to missions involving the exploration and

1. 2018 Draft Law on Space Activities, Commentaire des articles, p. 11.
2. Law of July 9, 1937 on Insurance Tax and Implementing Measures, RGBl I and RStBl 1937, as amended, https://ec.europa.eu/taxation_customs/tedb/taxDetails.html?id=398/1514764800#legal_baseTitle1 (accessed February 1, 2022).
3. Law of December 4, 1967 on Income Tax, as amended, Loi modifiée du 4 décembre 1967 concernant l'impôt sur le revenu, Texte coordonné en vigueur au 1er janvier 2021, https://impotsdirects.public.lu/dam-assets/fr/legislation/LIR/LIR2021.pdf (accessed February 1, 2022).

use of space resources governed by the Law of 20 July 2017 on the exploration and use of space resources, except for Article 15 and 16." This means that the exemption from the tax on insurance, and the eligibility to income tax benefits extends to the missions of exploration and use of space resources for commercial purposes.

III. EVALUATION

The exemption from the tax on contracts of insurance related to space objects and the eligibility for benefits related to the income tax are a welcome step for the space operators. They are an attractive concession for those that were operating space activities before the 2020 Law on Space Activities entered into force in Luxembourg, and for those for whom the beneficial situation would be lost. It is a specific provision that does not have any parallel in other space legislations. Other countries regulate the taxation of the contracts of insurance on space objects and the income related to space activities in their respective tax legislation.

Article 17 Transitional Provisions[*]

(1) Operators benefitting from a concession under Article 20 of the amended Law of 27 July 1991 on Electronic Media authorizing the performance of space activities and granted prior to the entry into force of the Law may continue to perform these activities without obtaining authorization under Article 5, paragraph 1, until 31 December 2022.
(2) The other operators that carry out already space activities on the date of entry into force of this Law shall be required to submit an application for authorization to the Minister within a period of nine months as from the entry into force of the Law and may continue to carry out these activities when awaiting the Minister's decision.
(3) Any operator continuing space activities at the time of entry into force of this Law shall have a period of two months to deliver the Minister the information provided for by Article 15 for the purposes of inclusion of the space objects in the Register.

I. DRAFTING HISTORY

To formulate the rules on the temporary scope of the Law and determine its retroactive effect was one of the most difficult political decisions of the legislator. At the time of submission of the 2018 Draft Law on Space Activities, there were some twenty satellites used by the SES Astra under a concession valid until December 31, 2021 and several new operators planning or carrying out space activities from Luxembourg. The question was how to approach those two groups. Should the concession remain valid after the entry of the Law into force and for how long? Do the new operators have to apply for authorization immediately after entry of the new Law into force, and if so, will they be able to operate on a provisional basis when awaiting the ministerial decision?

* Mahulena Hofmann

The very first working Draft on Law of Space Activities supposed that the act enters into force on March 1, 2018; therefore, this date was taken as a decisive criteria for the validity of the concessions. According to the original version of the than Article 19, the operators who carried out space activities based on a concession according to the 1991 Electronic Media Law[1] issued before March 1, 2018 were considered to continue legally their activities until December 31, 2021—the expiry of the last concession accorded to SES Astra. In this transitory period, SES was expected to apply for an authorization of its space activities according to the new Law. All other operators who performed their activities before March 1, 2018 were given a three-month deadline for applying the authorization. In this "waiting" period, their activities would be considered legal.

However, the legislative works took longer than envisaged and the entry into force of the new Law was postponed. Through this delay, the precise date—March 1, 2018—as a turning point of the legality of a space activity under the jurisdiction of Luxembourg—led to an occurrence of not two, but three categories of operators: First, the operators in possession of a concession issued before March 1, 2018; second, those who were not accorded any concession and were given a three months deadline after the entry of the Law into force, and third, those who were given a concession after March 1, 2018 not profiting from the transitory period until December 31, 2021. This result was criticized by the Chamber of Commerce, which was "astonished" why exactly March 1, 2018 was selected as a decisive date for the effect of diverse regimes. It recommended that the decisive date should not be any precise day but an abstract date of entering the Law into force.[2] Even more outspoken was the Conseil d'État: It categorized the position of those operators who were not in a possession of a concession issued before March 1, 2018 but later as "discriminatory." According to its Opinion, any objective reason for their different treatment—the lack of a transitory period—was missing.[3]

The new text of the Draft Law submitted in September 2020[4] reflected these views. Under the new numbering (Article 17), it replaced the decisive date of March 1, 2018 by the date of entering of the Law into force. Furthermore, it prolonged the transitory period of all operators holding a concession to December 31, 2022 and offered the operators without concession but already performing space activities a nine-month period instead of three to apply for the authorization.

Part 3 of Article 17 was not subject to any changes during the legislative works. The operators will have until two months after the Law enters into force to submit information necessary for inscribing their space objects into the National Registry of space objects established by Article 15 of the 2020 Law on Space Activities. According to the 2018 Commentary to the Articles, space objects which already deorbited or were placed in the graveyard orbit before entering the new Law into force are exempted from this duty.

1. 1991 Electronic Media Law, p. 1788.
2. Avis de la Chambre de commerce (November 19, 2018).
3. Avis du Conseil d'État (February 15, 2019) 16-17.
4. Amendements parlementaires (July 20, 2020).

II. INTERPRETATION

According to the Commentary of Articles to the last version of the Draft,[5] the present Article 17 contains transitory provisions for the validity of existing concessions and for raising applications for authorization by operators who already carry out space activities before the Law enters into force. The regime of concessions is regulated by the 1991 Electronic Media Law as amended,[6] and it provides in Article 20 that "nobody can operate a Luxemburgish satellite system without previously having obtained a concession, granted by the Government, based on a joint proposal from the Minister responsible for telecommunications and the Minister responsible for the media." A "Luxemburgish satellite system" is understood to be any system of one or more satellites using the satellite frequencies Luxembourg is entitled to exploit in accordance with the ITU framework which can be used either for broadcasting or any other service (Article 2 paragraph 27 of the Law). Such concession may consist of elements of exclusivity, particularly for the use of certain frequency bands or certain orbital positions (Article 20, paragraph 2). Any concession is accompanied by a book of binding obligations. If violated or not used, the concession can be withdrawn at any time, according to the conditions and arrangements laid down in the concession contract and the book of obligations. The activity of the concessionaire is monitored by one or more government commissionaires.

Next provision dealing with concessions is the Directive 2014/23/EU of February 26, 2012 on the Award of Concession Contracts which has been transposed into the legislation of Luxembourg in 2018. According to this Directive, "service concession" means a "contract for pecuniary interest concluded in writing by means of which one or more contracting authorities or contracting entities entrust the provision and the management of services other than the execution of works ... to one or more economic operators, the consideration of which consists either solely in the right to exploit the services that are subject of the contract or in that right together with payment."

According to Article 17 of the 2020 Law on Space Activities, an operator who was accorded a concession by the Government of Luxembourg before entry of the Law into force—January 1, 2021—can carry out its activities until December 31, 2022 without obtaining any new authorization. If the operator wishes to continue its activities after December 31, 2022, it will need a valid authorization issued according to the 2020 Law. The activities of operators who on January 1, 2021 already carried out space activities without a concession remained legal without any authorization for nine months after the entry of the Law into force—this means until October 1, 2021. They had to apply for an authorization during these nine months and wait for the result when performing their activities. Other operators—those without concession and those who started their activities on January 1, 2021 and later—must apply and wait for authorization according to the new Law.

5. Rapport de la Commission de l'Economie, de la Protection des Consommateurs et de l'Espace (December 2, 2020).
6. 1991 Electronic Media Law.

III. EVALUATION

The transitory provisions decided about the validity of the older concessions and the need to apply for authorization according to the 2020 Law on Space Activities. This regulation created three distinct regimes. First, the holders of a concession can continue their activities until December 31, 2022; after this date, their activity without any authorization would become illegal. To avoid the sanctions formulated in the Law, they must be in possession of an authorization from January 1, 2023. This is an obligation of result—to be in possession of an authorization.

Second, the activities of the operators active before the entry of the Law into force without concession were legal only until October 31, 2021. If they wanted to carry out their activities after October 31, 2021, they had to apply for an authorization until this very date. After submitting their application, their activity remained legal, as long as they were "awaiting the Minister's decision." No deadline for this decision is defined in the 2020 Law, and according to the exchange of views in the legislative process, the ordinary legislation of Luxembourg will apply. This is an obligation of measure—to apply for an authorization.

The third category of entities is represented by the new operators entering space activities after January 1, 2021. They had to apply for the authorization before the start of their activities, during the waiting period if they engage in space activities it would be illegal.

This differentiation may be explained by the sufficiently long time for the concession's holders to prepare the application for authorization on the one hand, and the need to legalize the activities of the already operating space companies as fast as possible on another hand. To unify the regimes of the operators with and without concession by opening a general transitory period until the end of 2022 would have led to a long period of legal instability.

The sanctions for carrying out an activity without authorization are tangible and correspond to those formulated in the 2017 Law on Space Resources. Article 5(1) of the 2020 Law provides that no operator can exercise any space activity without authorization. By "space activity" requiring such authorization, the Law means any activity consisting in launching or attempting to launch one or more space objects into outer space or in controlling one or more space objects or in using them during a stay in outer space, including the return to Earth, as well as any other activity taking place in outer space for which the Grand Duchy of Luxembourg is likely to be held internationally liable. The missing authorization is sanctioned in Article 14(1) by imprisonment from eight days to five years and a fine of EUR 5,000 to EUR 1,250,000 or just one of these penalties.

The 2020 Law did not abolish the 1991 Electronic Media Law. According to the Decree of December 5, 2018,[7] the Minister on Communications and Media remains responsible for the satellite systems of Luxembourg and the supervision of SES. This

7. Arrêté grand-ducal du 5 décembre portant constitution des Ministéres, Mémorial A N° 099.

means that the satellite systems that are using the frequencies registered by Luxembourg will further need a concession. This would be also in line with Article 5 of the 2020 Law on Space Activities, which does not exempt the operators from the obligation to obtain other approvals or authorization required.

The regulation of the transition from one legal regime to another is a usual approach for regulating the temporary scope of the laws, not only space laws. Similar provisions can be found in the 2011 Space Law of Austria (§15),[8] the 2006 Netherlands Space Activities Law (section 25),[9] and many others. An interesting difference between these laws and the one of Luxembourg is the fact that whereas they regulate activities of operators performing activities before their entering into force and the new ones, the Law of Luxembourg had to solve the legal status of those exercising space activities under the concessions issued under the 1991 Electronic Media Law.

8. Austrian Federal Law on the Authorisation of Space Activities and the Establishment of a National Space Registry (Austrian Outer Space Act, adopted by the National Space Council on December 6, 2011, entered into force on December 28, 2011).
9. Rules Concerning Space Activities and the Establishment of a Registry of Space Objects (Space Activities Act), June 13, 2006, as amended.

Article 18 Reference

The reference to this Law shall be made as follows: "Law of 15 December 2020 on space activity."

No commentary needed.

Chapter 3 Commentary on the 2020 Law on the Approval of the Registration Convention

Single Article*

The Convention on the Registration of Objects Launched into Outer Space, adopted by the General Assembly of the United Nations in New York on 12 November 1974 is approved.

We order this Law to be inserted in the Official Journal of the Grand Duchy of Luxembourg to be executed and observed by all concerned.

I. DRAFTING HISTORY

The first Draft of this Law was initiated by the Ministry of State, specifically the Service of Media and Communication,[1] and formally deposited to the Parliament by the Minister of Foreign and European Affairs on March 26, 2018,[2] several months before the deposition of the 2018 Draft Law on Space Activities of Luxembourg.[3] At that time, the Ministry of State was the entity responsible for space activities, and it also formulated the 2018 Draft Law on Space Activities.

Before ratifying the Registration Convention,[4] Luxembourg was State Party of the OST[5] and the Liability Convention.[6] The missing ratification of the Registration Convention did not mean, however, that the satellites procured by Luxembourg were not registered internationally. As explained in the Motives of the Draft,[7] the satellites launched especially by the company SAS ASTRA S.A. were voluntarily notified to the UN Secretary General on the basis of the UNGA Resolution 1721 B (XVI) of December 20, 1961. The adherence of Luxembourg to the Registration Convention did not change much on the substance of this flow of information delivered by Luxembourg authorities—above the information already submitted, only the appropriate designator

* Mahulena Hofmann
1. Currently, the Department of Media, Telecommunications and Digital Policy.
2. Parliamentary document No. 7270.
3. Parliamentary document No 7317/00 (June 12, 2018).
4. U.N.T.S., vol. 1023, No. 15020.
5. U.N.T.S., vol. 610, No. 8843.
6. U.N.T.S., vol. 961, No. 13810.
7. No 7270 of April 17, 2018.

of the space object and its registration number must be notified. However, the ratification modified the regime of registration from voluntary to an obligatory one.

The only precondition missing for the earlier ratification of the Registration Convention was the existence of a national registry of space objects launched into outer space required by the Article II of the Registration Convention. According to this provision, each launching State shall inform the UN Secretary General of the establishment of such registry. The legal basis for its setting up has been included in the 2018 Draft Law on Space Activities of Luxembourg deposited to the Parliament later, in June 2018.

This missing effective rule on a national registry was a critical issue in the Opinion of the Conseil d'État of May 8, 2018.[8] Therefore, according to the Opinion, the ratification of the Registration Convention had to be postponed until the 2020 Law on Space Activities, including this provision, has been adopted.[9] This happened as planned. The parliamentary voting on the 2020 Law on Space Activities took place on December 10, 2020, at the same day as the Law on Ratification of the Registration Convention.[10] On January 27, 2021, the depositary notification of the accession of the Registration Convention by Luxembourg to the Treaty Section of the United Nations followed.[11]

II. INTERPRETATION

The Registration Convention is a multilateral international treaty that enlarged the voluminous category of international treaties to which Luxembourg is a party. Luxembourg is a founding member of the United Nations, NATO, and the International Criminal Court. Luxembourg also accepts the jurisdiction of the International Court of Justice as compulsory, *ipso facto* and without the requirement of reciprocity, in any disputes arising after 1930, regarding situations or facts subsequent to its signature, except in cases where the parties have agreed or shall agree to have recourse to another procedure or to another method of pacific settlement.

As noted by *Jörg Gerkrath*, regarding the ratification of international treaties, Article 37 of the Constitution of Grand Duchy of Luxembourg provides that treaties are operative after having been approved by law and published in the form specified for the publication of laws. Drawing inspiration from the Belgian Constitution of 1831, Article 37 was last modified by the 1956 constitutional amendment. The amendment of 1956 did not alter the principle of the approval of international treaties by the Parliament; it only specified the form that this approval would take, by adding the requirement of approval by a law.[12]

8. No 7270[1] of May 8, 2018.
9. Journal officiel, Mémorial A, N° 1086, 15 décembre 2020.
10. Journal officiel, Mémorial A, N° 1087, 28 décembre 2020.
11. C.N.46.2021.
12. The Constitution of Luxembourg in the Context of EU Law and International Law as "Higher Law" (2019) https://link.springer.com/chapter/10.1007/978-94-6265-273-6_6#Fn87.

In its Opinion of July 10, 1956, the Conseil d'État underlined the distinction between the enforceability of the approving law and of the international treaty. They are two different procedures, which may take place simultaneously or separately, but both need to be compatible with the corresponding constitutional provisions. The Conseil d'État formulated one formal requirement, that of the publication of the approving law. This formal condition was fulfilled by the publication of the Law in the Official Journal of the Grand Duchy of December 28, 2020.[13]

Concerning the hierarchy of domestic and international norms, according to Gerkrath, Luxembourgish institutions and courts have adopted a progressive view on the position of international law in the national legal order, following a somewhat monistic approach, "should this term still be considered relevant." In the Constitution, there is no express reference to the legal status of international treaties in domestic law. However, the Conseil d'État and the Cour de Cassation have confirmed that in case of conflict between a rule of domestic law and a rule of international law that has direct effect in the domestic legal order, the rule of the international treaty shall prevail.

As the Registration Convention does not contain self-executing rules, a conflict between its international provisions and domestic regulations is hardly imaginable, especially in view of the fact that "the content of each registry and the conditions under which it is maintained shall be determined by the State of registry concerned" (Article II.3 of the Convention).

Each State Party is obliged to execute the provisions of ratified international treaties internationally in a good will. This happened very early after the adoption of the new Law. Article 15 of the 2020 Law on Space Activities required the operators to enter into the Register (in the English translation of the Law) space objects for which Luxembourg assumed a registration obligation under Article VIII of the Registration Convention (*see* Commentary on Article 15 in this volume). The operators have to provide the Minister responsible for space activities with information defined in this Article at the moment of their "initiative to launch or procure the launch of a space object," as well as about the changes or risk of changes in the parameters of the space object, particularly the danger of unintentional orbiting.

The Luxembourg public national registry of space objects can be found on the website of the Luxembourg Space Agency (LSA). It contains over fifty satellites, including those already in graveyard orbit or nonfunctional. The active satellites can be found on the website of UNOOSA under the Online Index of Objects Launched into Outer Space. For the companies, LSA issued a specific submission form for registering their satellites. According to Article 1 of the 2020 Law on Space Activities, operators are entities launching space objects from the territory of Luxembourg, or by means or installations under the control and jurisdiction of Luxembourg, or natural persons of Luxembourg nationality or legal persons established under Luxembourg law carrying out space activities out of Luxembourg. However, only those space objects will be registered in Luxembourg for "which the Grand Duchy shall assume a registration obligation under Article VIII of the Outer Space Treaty and Article II of the Registration

13. Journal officiel, Mémorial A, N° 1087, 28 décembre 2020.

Convention." This may be relevant in cases of more than one launching States. According to Article II (3) of the Registration Convention, if there are more launching States in respect of one space object, they shall jointly determine which one of them shall register the object.

III. EVALUATION

By acceding to the Registration Convention and adopting corresponding domestic provision for its domestic execution, Luxemburg fully legalized collecting defined information from the operators and delivering it to the international, UN Register. It can be said that it was done in an exemplary manner.

Not all countries have ratified the Registration Convention yet. As of January 1, 2021, 70 States ratified it, four international intergovernmental organizations have declared the acceptance of its rights and obligations, and three States have signed the treaty and have not yet ratified it.[14] Luxembourg[15] and Bahrain[16] acceded to these numbers during the year 2021.

Not all countries have adopted legal provisions for establishing a national registry of space objects. However, in those jurisdictions, where a specific space law was adopted, the establishment and organization of a national registry is one of its typical elements. As examples France,[17] Belgium,[18] The Netherlands,[19] Denmark,[20] Austria,[21] and Finland[22] can be mentioned.

14. Status of International Agreements relating to Activities in Outer Space as of January 1, 2021, A/AC.105/c.2/2021/CRP.10, www.unoosa.org.
15. C.N.46.2021.
16. C.N.211.2021.
17. 2008 French Space Act, Art. 12.
18. 2005 Belgian Space Law, Art. 14.
19. 2006 Netherlands Space Activities Law, Art. 11.
20. Danish Outer Space Act, Act No. 409 of May 11, 2016, Art. 5.
21. Austrian Federal Law on the Authorisation of Space Activities and the Establishment of a National Space Registry, 2011, §§ 9 and 10.
22. Act on Space Activities 63/2018, Art. 6.

Annexes

ANNEX I

Law of 20 July 2017 on the Exploration and Use of Space Resources

Mémorial A N° 674, 28 July 2017

This is the English translation of the French original text[1] *of the "Loi du 20 juillet 2017 sur l'exploration et l'utilisation des ressources de l'espace." The French version prevails.*

I Henri, Grand-Duc de Luxembourg, Duke of Nassau,
Having heard our Council of State;
On the consent of the Chamber of Deputies;
Having regard to the decision of the Chamber of Deputies of 13 July 2017 and that of the Council of State of 14 July 2017 declaring that no second vote is necessary;
Have ordered and order:

Article 1

Space resources are capable of being owned.

Article 2

(1) No person can explore or use space resources without holding a written mission authorization from the minister or ministers in charge of the economy and space activities (hereinafter "the ministers").
(2) No person shall be authorized to carry out the activity referred to in paragraph 1 either through another person or as an intermediary for the carrying out of such activity.
(3) The authorized operator may only carry out the activity referred to in paragraph 1 in accordance with the conditions of the authorization and the international obligations of Luxembourg.

1. *See* https://space-agency.public.lu/en/agency/legal-framework.html (last visit May 4, 2022).

(4) This Law shall not apply to satellite communications, orbital positions or the use of frequency bands.

Article 3

The authorization shall be granted to an operator for a mission of exploration and use of space resources for commercial purposes upon written application to the ministers.

Article 4

The authorization for a mission shall only be granted if the applicant is a public company limited by shares (*société anonyme*) or a corporate partnership limited by shares (*société en commandite par actions*) or a private limited liability company (*société à responsabilité limitée*) of Luxembourg law or a European Company (*société européenne*) having its registered office in Luxembourg.

Article 5

The authorization is personal and non-assignable.

Article 6

The application for authorization must be accompanied by all such information as may be useful for the assessment thereof as well as by a mission program.

Article 7

(1) The authorization shall be subject to the production of evidence showing the existence in Luxembourg of the central administration and of the registered office, including the administrative and accounting structures of the operator to be authorized.
(2) The operator to be authorized shall have a robust scheme of financial, technical and statutory procedures and arrangements through which the exploration and utilization mission, including the commercialisation of space resources are planned and implemented. The operator to be authorized shall furthermore have a robust internal governance scheme, which includes in particular a clear organisational structure with well defined, transparent and consistent lines of responsibility, effective processes to identify, manage, monitor and report the risks it is or might be exposed to, and adequate internal control mechanisms, including sound administrative and accounting procedures, as well as control and security arrangements for its technical systems and applications.
(3) The arrangements, processes, procedures and mechanisms referred to in this article shall be comprehensive and proportionate to the nature, scale and complexity of the risks inherent to the business model of the operator to be authorized as well as to the mission for which the authorization is sought.

Article 8

(1) The authorization shall be subject to the communication to the ministers of the identity of the shareholders or members, whether direct or indirect, natural or legal persons, that have direct or indirect holdings of at least 10 per cent of the capital or of the voting rights in the operator, and of the amount of such holdings or, if such 10 per cent threshold is not met, the identity of the twenty largest shareholders or members.

The authorization shall be refused if, taking into account the need to ensure a sound and prudent operation, the suitability of those shareholders or members is not satisfactory.

(2) The concept of sound and prudent operation is assessed in accordance with the following criteria:

a) the good repute of the operator to be authorized and the shareholders and members referred to in paragraph 1;

b) the good repute, knowledge, skills and experience of any member of the management body of the shareholders or members referred to in paragraph 1;

c) the financial soundness of the shareholders and members referred to in paragraph 1;

d) whether there are reasonable grounds to suspect that money laundering or terrorist financing is being or has been committed or attempted in relation to the proposed exploration mission or the proposed utilization of space resources or that such exploration mission or such utilization could increase the risk thereof.

The good repute of the members of the management body of the shareholders or members referred to in paragraph 1 shall be assessed in accordance with the terms of article 9, paragraph 1, second sentence.

Article 9

(1) The authorization shall be subject to the condition that the members of the management body of the operator shall at all times be of sufficiently good repute and possess sufficient knowledge, skills and experience to perform their duties. Such good repute shall be assessed on the basis of police records and of any evidence tending to show that the persons concerned are of good repute and offer every guarantee of irreproachable conduct.

(2) At least two persons must be responsible for the management of the operator. Those persons must be empowered to effectively determine the direction taken by the business. They must possess adequate professional experience by virtue of their having previously carried out similar activities at a high level of responsibility and autonomy in the space industry or in a related sector.

(3) Any change in the persons referred to in paragraph 1 shall be communicated in advance to the ministers. The ministers may request all such information as

may be necessary regarding the persons who may be required to fulfil the legal requirements with respect to good repute and professional experience. The ministers shall refuse the proposed change if these persons are not of adequate professional repute or do not have sufficient professional experience or where there are objective and demonstrable grounds for believing that the proposed change would pose a threat to the sound and prudent management of the operation.

(4) Granting the authorization implies that the members of the management body shall, on their own initiative, notify in writing and in a complete, coherent and comprehensive form, to the ministers any change regarding the substantial information on which the ministers based their investigation of the application for the authorization.

Article 10

(1) The application for the authorization must be accompanied by a risk assessment of the mission. It shall specify the coverage of these risks by personal financial means, by an insurance policy of an insurance undertaking not belonging to the same group than the operator to be authorized or by a guarantee of a credit institution not belonging to the same group than the operator to be authorized.

(2) The authorization shall be conditional upon the existence of financial bases that are appropriate to the risks associated with the mission.

Article 11

(1) The authorization shall be conditional on the operator to be authorized having its annual accounts audited by one or more *réviseurs d'entreprises agréés* who can show that they possess adequate professional experience.

(2) Any change in the *réviseurs d'entreprises agréés* must be authorized in advance by the ministers.

(3) The rules in respect of commissaires, which may form a supervisory board as laid down in the Law of 10 August 1915 on commercial companies, as amended, only apply to operators where the Law on commercial companies mandatorily prescribes it even if there is a *réviseur d'entreprise*.

Article 12

The authorization shall describe the manner in which the operator to be authorized fulfils the conditions of articles 6 to 11, paragraph 1. It may in addition include provisions on:

a) the activities to be carried on within the territory of the Grand Duchy or from such territory;
b) the limits that could be associated with the mission;
c) the modalities for the supervision of the mission;
d) the conditions for ensuring compliance by the operator to be authorized with its obligations;

Article 13

For each application for an authorization, a fee shall be set by the ministers in order to cover the administrative expenses incurred in relation to the processing of the application. Such fee shall range from 5.000 to 500.000 euros depending on the complexity of the application and the amount of work involved.

A Grand-Ducal regulation shall determine the procedure applicable to the collection of such fee.

Article 14

(1) The authorization shall be withdrawn if the conditions for the granting thereof are no longer met.
(2) The authorization shall be withdrawn if the operator does not make use thereof within thirty-six months of it being granted, renounces to it or has ceased to carry out his business for the preceding six months.
(3) The authorization shall furthermore be withdrawn if it has been obtained through false statements or through any other irregular means.

Article 15

The ministers are in charge of the continuous supervision of the missions for which an authorization has been granted.

Article 16

The operator that is granted an authorization for a mission is fully responsible for any damage caused at the occasion of the mission, including at the occasion of all preparatory works and duties.

Article 17

The granting of an authorization for a mission does not dispense from the need to obtain other approvals or authorizations.

Article 18

(1) Any person who contravenes or attempts to contravene the provisions of article 2 shall be punished by a term of imprisonment of between eight days

and five years and a fine of between 5.000 and 1.250.000 euros or either one of those penalties.

(2) Any person who contravenes or attempts to contravene the provisions of articles 5, 9 paragraph 3 subparagraph 1, 11 paragraph 1 or 2 or that contravenes the terms and conditions of the authorization shall be punished by a term of imprisonment of between eight days and one year and a fine of between 1.250 and 500.000 euros or either one of those penalties.

(3) Without prejudice to paragraphs 1 and 2, the court to which the matter is being referred, may declare the discontinuance of an operation contravening the provisions of the present law, under a penalty the maximum of which shall not exceed 1.000.000 euros per day of infringement found.

We order this Law to be inserted in the Official Journal of the Grand Duchy of Luxembourg to be executed and observed by all concerned.

Minister of Economy, Étienne Schneider	Cabasson, 20 July 2017 Henri

ANNEX II

Law of 15 December 2020 on Space Activities

amending:

1 **the amended Law of 9 July 1937 on Insurance Tax known as "Versicherungssteuergesetz";**
2 **the amended Law of 4 December 1967 on Income Tax**

Mémorial A N° 1086, 28 December 2020

This is the English translation of the French original text[1] *of the "Loi du 15 décembre 2020 portant sur les activités spatiales." The French version prevails.*

I Henri, Grand-Duc de Luxembourg, Duke of Nassau,

Having heard our Council of State;

On the consent of the Chamber of Deputies;

Having regard to the decision of the Chamber of Deputies of 10 December 2020 and that of the Council of State of 15 December 2020 declaring that no second vote is necessary;

Have ordered and order:

Chapter 1 – Scope of application and general provisions

Article 1

This Law shall apply to space activities carried out:

1. by an operator, whatever the nationality thereof, from the territory of the Grand Duchy of Luxembourg or by means of installations, whether movable or

1. *See* https://space-agency.public.lu/en/agency/legal-framework/Lawspaceactivities.html (last visit May 4, 2022).

immovable, under the control and jurisdiction of the Grand Duchy of Luxembourg; or

2. in the territory of a foreign State or an area not subject to the sovereignty of a State by natural persons of Luxembourg nationality or by legal persons established under Luxembourg law.

This Law shall not apply to missions involving the exploration and use of space resources governed by the Law of 20 July 2017 on the exploration and use of space resources, except for Articles 15 and 16, paragraph 2.

Article 2

For the application of this Law the following should be understood:

1. "space activity": any activity consisting in launching or attempting to launch one or more space objects into outer space or in controlling one or more space objects or in using them during a stay in outer space, including the return to Earth, as well as any other activity taking place in outer space for which the Grand Duchy of Luxembourg is likely to be held internationally liable;
2. "Liability Convention": the Convention on International Liability for Damage Caused by Space Objects done in London, Moscow and Washington on 29 March 1972;
3. "damage": any harm to persons, property, public health or the environment directly caused by a space object within the scope of a space activity, excluding the consequences of use of the signal emitted by that object for users;
4. "space object": any object launched or intended to be launched into outer space, the component parts of such object and its launch vehicle and parts thereof;
5. "operator": any person who, on his own behalf, carries out or undertakes any space activity, alone or jointly with others;
6. "qualifying holding": the holding in an operator, either directly or indirectly, of at least 10% of the capital or voting rights, or any other possibility of exercising considerable influence over the management of that operator;
7. "Space Treaty": Treaty on Principles Governing the Activities of States in the Exploration and Use of Outer Space, including the Moon and Other Celestial Bodies, done in London, Moscow and Washington on 27 January 1967.

Article 3

The authorized operator may only carry out space activity in accordance with the conditions of its authorization and the international obligations of the Grand Duchy of Luxembourg.

Article 4

An operator that has obtained authorization for a space activity shall be fully liable for any damage caused during its space activity, including during any preparation works and duties.

Chapter 2 – Authorization of space activity

Article 5

(1) No operator can exercise any space activity without being previously authorized by the Minister in charge of the space policy and legislation, hereinafter the “Minister”.
(2) Obtaining the authorization referred to in paragraph 1 shall not exempt the operator from the need to obtain other approvals or authorizations required.
(3) Any authorization to carry out space activity shall take the form of a ministerial order and shall be granted on written application sent to the Minister.
(4) For each application for authorization, a fee shall be fixed by the Minister to cover the administrative costs incurred in dealing with the application. This fee shall vary between 5,000 euros and 500,000 euros depending on the complexity of the application and the volume of work.
A Grand-Ducal regulation shall determine the procedure applicable for collection of the fee.
(5) Authorization shall be personal and non-assignable, subject to Article 12.

Article 6

(1) An operator to be authorized shall provide evidence of the existence in the Grand Duchy of Luxembourg of its registered office and its central administration, including the administrative and accounting structure. An operator to be authorized shall have a robust system of financial, technical and legal procedures and methods by which space activity shall be planned and implemented. It shall also have a robust system of internal governance comprising in particular a clear organizational structure with well-defined, transparent and consistent lines of responsibilities, effective processes for the detection, management, control and reporting of risks to which it is or could be exposed, adequate internal control mechanisms, including sound administrative and accounting procedures as well as control and security mechanisms for its technical systems and applications.
The systems, processes, procedure and mechanisms referred to in the previous paragraph shall be exhaustive and adapted to the nature, scale and complexity of the risks inherent in the business model of the operator to be authorized as well as the space activity for which authorization is requested.

The members of the operator's governing body shall have the honourability, knowledge, skills and experience required to exercise their duties at all times. Honourability shall be assessed based on judicial records and all aspects able to establish that the persons referred to have professional honourability and present all the guarantees of irreproachable activity.

Any change in the persons referred to in the foregoing paragraph must be notified to the Minister in advance.

There must be at least two persons responsible for the management of the operator and they must be authorized to determine the direction of space activity effectively. They must have gained adequate professional experience by having already carried out similar activities with a high level of responsibility and independence in the space sector or a related sector.

(2) Authorization shall be subject to notification to the Minister of the identity of the shareholders or partners, whether direct or indirect, natural or legal persons, who have a qualifying holding, and of the amount of such holdings or, if the threshold provided for in Article 2, point 6, is not reached, of the identity of the twenty main shareholders or partners.

Authorization shall be refused if, taking into account the need to guarantee a sound and prudent operation, the capacity of the aforesaid shareholders or partners is not satisfactory.

The concept of sound and prudent operation shall be assessed in light of the following criteria:

1. the professional honourability of the operator to be authorized and of the shareholders and partners referred to in section 1;
2. the honourability, knowledge, skills and experience of every member of the governing body of the shareholders and partners referred to in section 1;
3. the financial soundness of the shareholders and partners referred to in section 1;
4. the existence of reasonable grounds for suspecting that a transaction involving or an attempt at money laundering or terrorist financing is in progress or has taken place in relation to the space activity envisaged or that such activity could increase the risk thereof.

The honourability of the members of the governing body of the shareholders or partners referred to in section 1 shall be assessed according to the terms of Article 6, paragraph 1, section 4, second sentence.

(3) Any change in the persons referred to in paragraph 1, section 4, must be notified to the Minister in advance. The Minister may request any information necessary on the persons that may be required to fulfil the legal conditions of professional honourability or experience. The Minister shall object to the change envisaged if such persons do not have adequate professional honourability or adequate professional experience or if there are demonstrable objective reasons for considering that the change envisaged risks jeopardizing a sound and prudent operation.

(4) Applications for authorization must be accompanied by an assessment of the risks of space activity. They shall specify the coverage of such risks by the operator's own financial resources, by an insurance policy arranged with an insurance company not belonging to the same group as the operator to be authorized or by a guarantee issued by a credit institution not belonging to the same group as the operator to be authorized.

Authorization shall be subject to the existence of financial bases appropriate to the risks associated with space activity.

(5) Authorization shall be subject to the condition that the operator to be authorized assigns the audit of its annual accounting documents to one or more approved auditors (*réviseurs d'entreprises agréés*) providing evidence of adequate professional experience.

Any change in the approved company auditors (*réviseurs d'entreprises agréés*) must be authorized by the Minister in advance.

The institution of *commissaires* who may form a supervisory board, provided for by the amended Law of 10 August 1915 on commercial companies, shall only apply to operators if required by the Law on commercial companies, even if there is a company auditor (*un réviseur d'entreprises)*.

Article 7

Any application for authorization must be accompanied by all useful information for the assessment thereof as well as an activity programme. The standard content of an application for authorization may be established by a Grand-Ducal regulation.

Article 8

(1) The authorization shall describe the way in which the operator to be authorized satisfies the conditions of Articles 6 and 7. It may also contain provisions on:
   1. the activities having to be carried out in or from the territory of the Grand Duchy of Luxembourg;
   2. the limits to which the space activity could be subject;
   3. the procedure for supervision of space activity;
   4. the conditions serving to ensure that the operator to be authorized fulfils its obligations.

(2) The authorizations shall be subject to payment by the operator of an annual fee to the State. The annual fee shall be between 2,000 euros and 50,000 euros depending on the costs incurred by supervision, and it may be increased by experts' expenses incurred without being able to exceed 500,000 euros per annum. A Grand-Ducal regulation shall determine the procedure applicable for collecting the annual fee.

(3) The granting of authorization shall imply for the operator the obligation to notify the Minister voluntarily, in writing and in a complete, consistent and

comprehensible manner of any substantial change in the information used by the Minister to examine the application for authorization.

Article 9

(1) Authorization shall be withdrawn if:
   1. the conditions for granting it are no longer fulfilled;
   2. the authorization was obtained by means of false declarations or by any other irregular means;
   3. the operator does not make use of it within a period of thirty-six months as from the granting thereof, and abandons or has ceased to carry out its activity in the last six months.

(2) In the event of the withdrawal of authorization, the Minister shall take all necessary measures to prevent the space activities for which the authorization was withdrawn from affecting the safety of persons or property or the environment or causing an increased risk of international liability for the Luxembourg State. The Minister may request the services of third parties for these purposes or transfer control over the space object to another operator to ensure the continuity of flight operations and guidance and, if necessary, to ensure re-orbiting or de-orbiting, even if such operations risk giving rise to the loss or destruction of the space object.

Article 10

The Minister shall keep a public register of authorizations granted under this law, according to the terms established by the Grand-Ducal regulation.

Chapter 3 – Supervision of space activities

Article 11

Operators authorized to carry out space activity under Article 5 shall be subject to the Minister's continuous supervision.

Chapter 4 – Transfer of space activities

Article 12

(1) Unless authorized by the Minister in advance, any transfer to a third party of the space activities authorized or of real or personal rights, including guarantee rights, involving the transfer of actual control over the space object, shall be prohibited.

For the purposes of this article, "actual control" shall be deemed to mean: the authority exercised over the activation of the means of control or telecommand and, where appropriate, the associated monitoring devices, required for the execution of the launch, flight operation or guidance activities of one or more space objects.

(2) Requests for authorization to transfer shall be made jointly by the transferor operator and the transferee operator.

(3) All the provisions applicable to the authorization referred to in Article 6, paragraph 1, sections 2 et seq. and in paragraphs 2 to 4 shall apply to the authorization to transfer.

(4) When the transferee operator is not established in the Grand Duchy of Luxembourg, the Minister shall refuse transfer authorization in the absence of a special agreement with the State of which the transferee operator is a national or which has international liability for the space activities thereof and which guarantees the Luxembourg State against any recourse brought against it on account of its international liability or for compensation for loss or damage.

Chapter 5 – Change of control

Article 13

(1) Any natural or legal person that has taken the decision to acquire or increase, either directly or indirectly, a qualifying holding in an operator, resulting in the proportion of capital units or voting rights held amounting to or exceeding the thresholds of 20%, 30% or 50% or such operator becoming its subsidiary, shall inform the Minister of its intention in advance in writing.

(2) Any natural or legal person that has taken the decision to transfer, either directly or indirectly, a qualifying holding or to reduce its qualifying holding so that the proportion of capital units or voting rights held amounts to less than the thresholds of 20%, 30% or 50% or the operator ceases to be its subsidiary, shall inform the Minister of its intention in advance in writing.

(3) The potential acquirer of a qualifying holding shall provide the Minister with information indicating the amount of the holding envisaged. The Minister shall publish a list specifying the information required to assess the notification having to be submitted to him at the time of notification.

(4) If the influence exercised by a potential acquirer referred to in paragraph 3 is likely to be exercised to the detriment of sound and prudent operation by the operator, the Minister shall object thereto or take appropriate measures to end such a situation.

For the purposes of section 1, the Minister may suspend exercise of the voting rights attached to the shares or units held by the shareholders or partners concerned.

When a holding is acquired despite the Minister's objection, the Minister may suspend exercise of the corresponding voting rights or request the nullity or invalidation of the votes cast.

The Minister may take the same measures in respect of natural or legal persons that fail to observe the obligation to provide prior information provided for by this article.

The measures provided for in this paragraph may be the subject of an appeal for reversal before the administrative court ruling on the substance of the case.

(5) Every operator shall be required to inform the Minister, as soon as it becomes aware thereof, of any acquisitions or transfers of qualifying holdings in its capital.

Chapter 6 – Sanctions

Article 14

(1) Anyone who has infringed or attempted to infringe Articles 3, 5, paragraph 1, or 12, paragraph 1 or paragraph 4 shall be penalized with imprisonment from eight days to five years and a fine of €5,000 euros to 1,250,000 euros or just one of these penalties.

(2) Anyone who has infringed or attempted to infringe the provisions of Articles 5, paragraph 5, 6, paragraph 1, section 5, 6, paragraph 5, sections 1 and 2, or the terms of the authorization, respectively, shall be penalized by imprisonment from eight days to one year and a fine of 1,250 euros to 500,000 euros or just one of these penalties.

(3) Without prejudice to paragraphs 1 and 2, the court applied to may pronounce termination of the space activity contrary to the provision of this Law under a penalty of a fine whose maximum amount may not exceed 1,000,000 euros per day of infringement established.

Chapter 7 – Registration of space objects launched

Article 15

(1) A National Register of Space Objects, hereinafter referred to as the "Register" is set up by the Minister in charge of Space Policy and Legislation. The space objects for which the Grand Duchy of Luxembourg shall assume a registration obligation under Article VIII of the Space Treaty and Article II of the Convention on Registration of Objects Launched into Outer Space, adopted by the United Nations General Assembly in New York on 12 November 1974, shall be entered in the Register. This Register shall be public.

(2) An operator taking the initiative to launch or to procure the launch of a space object into outer space must provide the Minister with all information allowing to identify the space object, its launch and the position it has to occupy in outer space, including the nodal period, inclination, apogee,

perigee and in particular the launching date and territory or place, the main parameters of the orbit and the general function of the space object.

(3) The operator must inform the Minister without delay of any change or risk of change in the parameters of the space object, particularly the danger of unintentional de-orbiting.

(4) If the space object is marked by a registration indication or number, the operator shall inform the Minister thereof.

Chapter 8 – Amending, transitional and final provisions

Article 16

(1) Article 4 of the amended Law of 9 July 1937 on insurance tax, known as "Versicherungssteuergesetz", shall be amended as follows:
   1. The figure "8." is inserted before the words "for contracts of insurance covering ships";
   2. A point 9 is added worded as follows: "9. for contracts of insurance related to space objects falling within the scope of application of Article 15 of the Law of 15 December 2020 on space activity."

(2) Article 152*bis* of the amended Law of 4 December 1967 on income tax is amended as follows:
   1. In section 1, the terms "paragraphs 2 and 7" shall be replaced by the terms "sections 2 and 7".
   2. A section 1a is inserted, worded as follows: "The condition indicated in section 1 shall not apply to space objects as defined in Article 2, point 4, of the Law of 15 December 2020 on space activity."

Article 17

(1) Operators benefiting from a concession under Article 20 of the amended Law of 27 July 1991 on electronic media authorizing the performance of space activities and granted prior to the entry into force of the Law may continue to perform these activities without obtaining authorization under Article 5, paragraph 1, until 31 December 2022.

(2) The other operators that already carry out space activities on the date of entry into force of this Law shall be required to submit an application for authorization to the Minister within a period of nine months as from the entry into force of the Law and may continue to carry out these activities while awaiting the Minister's decision.

(3) Any operator continuing space activity at the time of entry into force of this Law shall have a period of two months to deliver to the Minister the information provided for by Article 15 for the purposes of inclusion of the space objects in the Register.

Article 18

The reference to this Law shall be made as follows: "Law of 15 December 2020 on space activities".

We order this Law to be inserted in the Official Journal of the Grand Duchy of Luxembourg to be executed and observed by all concerned.

Minister of Economy,
Franz Fayot

Château de Berg, 15 December 2020
Henri

Annex III

Law of 15 December 2020 on the Law Approving the Convention on the Registration of Objects Launched into Outer Space, Adopted by the General Assembly of the United Nations in New York on 12 November 1974

Mémorial A N° 1087, 28 December 2020

This is the English translation of the French original text of the Loi du 15 décembre 2020 portant approbation de la Convention sur l'immatriculation des objets lancés dans l'espace extra-atmosphérique, adoptée par l'Assemblée générale des Nations unies, à New York, le 12 novembre 1974. The French version prevails.

I, Henri, Grand Duke of Luxembourg, Duke of Nassau,
Having heard our Council of State;
On the consent of the Chamber of Deputies;
Having regard to the decision of the Chamber of Deputies of 10 December 2020 and of the Council of State of 15 December 2020 declaring that no second vote is necessary,
Have ordered and order:

Single Article

The Convention on the Registration of Objects Launched into Outer Space, adopted by the General Assembly of the United Nations in New York on 12 November 1974 is approved.

We order this Law to be inserted in the Official Journal of the Grand Duchy of Luxembourg to be executed and observed by all concerned.

Minister of Foreign and European Affairs
Jean Asselborn

Chateau de Berg, 15 December 2020
Henri

Minister of Economy,
Franz Fayot

Index

M

N

O

P

Q

R

S

AEROSPACE LAW AND POLICY SERIES

1. Erwin von den Steinen, *National Interest and International Aviation*, 2006 (ISBN 90-411-2455-1).
2. Ludwig Weber, *International Civil Aviation Organisation: An Introduction*, 2007 (ISBN 978-90-411-2622-1).
3. Niels van Antwerpen, *Cross-Border Provision of Air Navigation Services with Specific Reference to Europe: Safeguarding Transparent Lines of Responsibility and Liability*, 2008 (ISBN 978-90-411-2688-7).
4. Brian F. Havel, *Beyond Open Skies: A New Regime for International Aviation*, 2009 (ISBN 978-90-411-2389-3).
5. Jiefang Huang, *Aviation Safety through the Rule of Law: ICAO's Mechanisms and Practices*, 2009 (ISBN 978-90-411-3115-7).
6. Marian Hoeks, *Multimodal Transport Law: The Law Applicable to the Multimodal Contract for the Carriage of Goods*, 2010 (ISBN 978-90-411-3246-8).
7. George N. Tompkins, Jr., *Liability Rules Applicable to International Air Transportation as Developed by the Courts in the United States: From Warsaw 1929 to Montreal 1999*, 2010 (ISBN 978-90-411-2646-7).
8. Daniel Calleja Crespo and Pablo Mendes de Leon (eds), *Achieving the Single European Sky: Goals and Challenges*, 2011 (ISBN 978-90-411-3730-2).
9. Donal Patrick Hanley, *Aircraft Operating Leasing: A Legal and Practical Analysis in the Context of Public and Private International Air Law, Third Edition*, 2022 (ISBN 978-94-035-4030-6).
10. Mikołaj Ratajczyk, *Regional Aviation Safety Organisations: Enhancing Air Transport Safety through Regional Cooperation*, 2015 (ISBN 978-90-411-5861-1).
11. Benjamyn I. Scott (ed.), *The Law of Unmanned Aircraft Systems, Second Edition*, 2022 (ISBN 978-94-035-4573-8).
12. Stamatis Varsamos, *Airport Competition Regulation in Europe*, 2016 (ISBN 978-90-411-6831-3).
13. Katarzyna Malinowska, *Space Insurance: International Legal Aspects*, 2017 (ISBN 978-90-411-6784-2).
14. John Milligan, *European Union Competition Law in the Airline Industry*, 2017 (ISBN 978-90-411-6618-0).

15. Dejian Kong, *Civil Liability for Damage Caused by Global Navigation Satellite System*, 2019 (ISBN 978-94-035-1171-9).
16. Pablo Mendes de Leon and Niall Buissing (eds), *Behind and Beyond the Chicago Convention: The Evolution of Aerial Sovereignty*, 2019 (ISBN 978-94-035-1131-3).
17. Neta Palkovitz, *Regulating a Revolution: Small Satellites and the Law of Outer Space*, 2019 (ISBN 978-94-035-1762-9).
18. Federico Bergamasco, Roberto Cassar, Rada Popova & Benjamyn I. Scott, *Cybersecurity: Key Legal Considerations for the Aviation and Space Sectors*, 2020 (ISBN 978-94-035-0110-9).
19. Luis Fernando Fiallos Pazmiño, *The International Civil Operations of Unmanned Aircraft Systems under Air Law*, 2021 (ISBN 978-94-035-2854-0).
20. Merinda E. Stewart, *Freedom of Overflight: A Study of Coastal State Jurisdiction in International Airspace*, 2021 (ISBN 978-94-035-3804-4).
21. Cyril-Igor Grigorieff, *Uniformity and Fragmentation of the 1999 Montreal Convention on International Air Carrier Liability*, 2022 (ISBN 978-94-035-3732-0).
22. Mahulena Hofmann, P.J. Blount, Gabrielle Leterre, Antonino Salmeri & Laetitia Zarkan, *Space Legislation of Luxembourg: A Commentary*, 2022 (ISBN 978-94-035-4381-9).

www.ingramcontent.com/pod-product-compliance
Ingram Content Group UK Ltd.
Pitfield, Milton Keynes, MK11 3LW, UK
UKHW020844290926
15470UKWH00004B/1537

9 789403 543819